Language and Aging in Multilingual Contexts

BILINGUAL EDUCATION AND BILINGUALISM
Series Editors: Professor Nancy H. Hornberger, *University of Pennsylvania, Philadelphia, USA* and Professor Colin Baker, *University of Wales, Bangor, Wales, Great Britain*

Recent Books in the Series
World English: A Study of its Development
  Janina Brutt-Griffler
Power, Prestige and Bilingualism: International Perspectives on Elite Bilingual Education
  Anne-Marie de Mejía
Identity and the English Language Learner
  Elaine Mellen Day
Language and Literacy Teaching for Indigenous Education: A Bilingual Approach
  Norbert Francis and Jon Reyhner
The Native Speaker: Myth and Reality
  Alan Davies
Language Socialization in Bilingual and Multilingual Societies
  Robert Bayley and Sandra R. Schecter (eds)
Language Rights and the Law in the United States: Finding our Voices
  Sandra Del Valle
Continua of Biliteracy: An Ecological Framework for Educational Policy, Research, and Practice in Multilingual Settings
  Nancy H. Hornberger (ed.)
Languages in America: A Pluralist View (2nd edition)
  Susan J. Dicker
Trilingualism in Family, School and Community
  Charlotte Hoffmann and Jehannes Ytsma (eds)
Multilingual Classroom Ecologies
  Angela Creese and Peter Martin (eds)
Negotiation of Identities in Multilingual Contexts
  Aneta Pavlenko and Adrian Blackledge (eds)
Beyond the Beginnings: Literacy Interventions for Upper Elementary English Language Learners
  Angela Carrasquillo, Stephen B. Kucer and Ruth Abrams
Bilingualism and Language Pedagogy
  Janina Brutt-Griffler and Manka Varghese (eds)
Language Learning and Teacher Education: A Sociocultural Approach
  Margaret R. Hawkins (ed.)
The English Vernacular Divide: Postcolonial Language Politics and Practice
  Vaidehi Ramanathan
Bilingual Education in South America
  Anne-Marie de Mejía (ed.)
Teacher Collaboration and Talk in Multilingual Classrooms
  Angela Creese
Words and Worlds: World Languages Review
  Martí, P. Ortega, I. Idiazabal, A. Barreña, P. Juaristi, C. Junyent, B. Uranga, E. Amorrortu

For more details of these or any other of our publications, please contact:
Multilingual Matters, Frankfurt Lodge, Clevedon Hall,
Victoria Road, Clevedon, BS21 7HH, England
http://www.multilingual-matters.com

BILINGUAL EDUCATION AND BILINGUALISM 53
Series Editors: Nancy H. Hornberger and Colin Baker

Language and Aging in Multilingual Contexts

Kees de Bot and Sinfree Makoni

MULTILINGUAL MATTERS LTD
Clevedon • Buffalo • Toronto

Dedicated to Mai Tino for managing Tendayi with grace

Library of Congress Cataloging in Publication Data
De Bot, Kees.
Language and Aging in Multilingual Contexts/Kees de Bot and Sinfree Makoni.
Bilingual Education and Bilingualism: 53
Includes bibliographical references and index.
1. Multilingualism. 2. Aging. I. Makoni, Sinfree. II. Title. III. Series.
P115.D4 2005
306.44'6–dc22   2005009680

British Library Cataloguing in Publication Data
A catalogue entry for this book is available from the British Library.

ISBN 1-85359-841-0/EAN 978-1-85359-841-8 (hbk)
ISBN 1-85359-840-2/EAN 978-1-85359-840-1 (pbk)

Multilingual Matters Ltd
UK: Frankfurt Lodge, Clevedon Hall, Victoria Road, Clevedon BS21 7HH.
USA: UTP, 2250 Military Road, Tonawanda, NY 14150, USA.
Canada: UTP, 5201 Dufferin Street, North York, Ontario M3H 5T8, Canada.

Typeset by Archetype-IT Ltd (http://www.archetype-it.com).
Printed and bound in Great Britain by the Cromwell Press Ltd.

Contents

Preface

This book has a long history. The authors' interest in the topic dates from many years ago, and they have taken quite a lot of time to turn their ideas into something which became this book in the end. Over the years we have had long and intensive discussions with many colleagues in the field. One particularly important and stimulating event was the conference on Sociocultural Theory and Language Learning that took place at Penn State University in 2001. We are grateful to all those colleagues who were willing to share their views with us. We are also indebted to Margie Berns for inviting the first author to present a plenary lecture on language and aging at the 2002 Congress of the American Association of Applied Linguistics. This invitation gave us the inspiration to expand the topic and stimulated our attempts to develop an applied linguistic perspective on language and aging. The first author is also indebted to the Max Planck Institute for Psycholinguistics in Nijmegen for its hospitality during a sabbatical in 2002 during which a considerable part of this book was conceptualized. We would also like to thank the Africana Research Center at Pennsylvania State University for their support. Lorraine Obler helped us restructure the book in significant ways and we are indebted to her for her support.

Finally we are grateful to Marjan Scholman, Willemijn Muggen and Xingren Xu for their help with the bibliography and proofreading.

Kees de Bot
Groningen, November 2004

Sinfree Makoni
College Town, November 2004

Chapter 1

Introduction: Language, Aging and Multilingualism

While not all of us may be second language learners, or have participated in bilingual education or have lost a foreign language we once knew, we all become old, provided we don't die prematurely. And most of us at some stage in our life are confronted with the fact that our parents, or even our brothers and sisters, become old and with the fact that not all of our relatives and friends remain completely healthy mentally and physically until they die. In this book we want to focus on one aspect: language in aging.

Before going into the relation between language and aging, we need for a moment to stop and think what aging actually is. If we look at pictures of our own great-grandparents, we are likely to see pictures of very old people, the way they look, the way they dress. If we happen to have information on their real age, we will probably find out that those very old people are actually in their late 50s or early 60s. Even your own parents probably looked old when they were that age. In a sense they were older than we are, because in many ways, our healthcare system has led to increased life expectancies and more years in good health. Our attitudes towards aging have changed. There is still respect for old age, but we try to avoid being old, being seen as old or feeling old, as long as we can.

So what is aging? It is a generally accepted position in gerontology nowadays that age is an index variable that doesn't explain anything. It is probably best to define aging as a change on three interacting dimensions: biological, psychological and social. No one is denying that there are physical changes in our body over time, but they have their impact in different ways in different individuals. The risk of mental and physical decline increases more or less with age in the larger population, but strictly speaking grouping of individuals on the basis of age in order to learn more about aging is inappropriate. As we will argue later on, the effects of aging result from an interaction between these three dimensions, and only a part of the changes in one of these three dimensions can actually be compensated for by interventions in the other two dimensions.

Related to these issues is the problem of defining what constitutes normal healthy aging and pathological aging. As will be clarified in various chapters, no instrument is able to make a clear-cut distinction between the two. We take the position that pathology/non-pathology is a scale and that individuals have a position on that scale. As in most research on aging and dementia, we will look mainly at 'clear' cases and avoid the twilight zone in the middle up to a point. Maybe there is a place for language and assessment in that zone: maybe language can serve as an indicator of early dementia. We will present some research that suggests that this may be the case. A particularly difficult area is what has been called depressive dementia, i.e. syndromes that on the behavioral level are similar to degenerative dementia of the Alzheimer type but that are caused by depression and generally reversible. A treatment of that type is beyond the scope of the present book. An overview of research on language from this perspective can be found in Emery (1999).

There are other ways of looking at old age, not as a stage in life in which almost everything is worse than in earlier stages and the emphasis is on decline and on what is missing, but as a stage in its own right, just as childhood is not an incomplete version of adulthood. In this stage other matters become important; there is a different perception of time, work, maybe religion, certainly meaning of life. We can study this stage in itself and look at its inherent characteristics without reference to norms from an earlier stage. The two perspectives, aging as decline and aging as acceptance and fulfillment, lead to totally different questions we may want to answer in our research. While most of the research has been done from the decline perspective, we will argue for a perspective that looks at language and aging from the life-span development. In this perspective language development (or any development) does not stop at age 16 or 18 or whatever ages have been proposed for full language acquisition, but continues to develop over the life span. Due to changes in life, education, jobs, relationships or hobbies, people continue to learn new aspects of their languages. In such a perspective development includes not only growth, but also decline as part of the normal process.

Equally fundamental questions can be asked with respect to what, in this specific context, 'language' is. There is little point in going into this deep philosophical question in the context of the present book, but one needs to take a position on a number of issues in order to discuss the relation between language and aging. Here, language use is seen as very advanced and complex skilled behavior. Skills develop with use, and decline with non-use. The basic skills may be quite resistant to decline, like our abilities to ride a bicycle or swim. Once we've learned them we don't forget the basics. But for doing more advanced things quickly and properly, a lot of exercise is needed. In a way using language is like top sports: it is complex, extremely fast and calls for integration of many different skills. The complex parts of that skill need to be trained regularly to maintain them, otherwise they atrophy and fade, and are difficult to reactivate.

Language is not seen as a separate skill or capacity in our cognitive system. It is linked to and interacts with other subsystems, such as perception, memory and emotion. In the chapters that follow we will try to show how different components of language change over time with aging. Throughout this book, language will be presented as a complex dynamic system, and notions from dynamic systems theory will be used to show how language development across the life span fits in more general theories on development. The main thrust of this approach is that the language system is always changing and that it is always in interaction with other systems and dependent on input and use for maintenance.

The third main issue in the introductory chapters will be the role of memory in language use. Different types of memory play specific roles in language use. Many things have to be remembered in speaking and listening: the setting, the goal of the conversation, characteristics of the interlocutors, the topic, who said what and when. In the production and perception processes, there is temporary storage of outcomes of subprocesses. In particular working memory is crucial in language processing. The role of working memory is one of the most hotly debated issues in psycholinguistics at the moment, and though we will try to clarify the many functions of memory systems, a full treatment of this complex issue is beyond the scope of the present book.

The fourth issue has to do with multilingualism. As in the rest of the population, the majority of the world's elderly people are bilingual or multilingual. Multilingualism is defined here as being proficient to a certain degree in more than one language. In some definitions only people who grow up speaking more than one language qualify, but this definition has been discarded for a while now. There is no absolute measure for being bilingual. It does not amount to a given number of words or grammar rules in another language or the ability to carry out certain communicative activities in that language. In his definition of bilingual aphasia, Paradis (1987) takes 400 hours of formal instruction as the lower limit. How that translates to non-instructed acquisition is not really clear but participating in a foreign society and language for more than a few weeks should be enough. To what extent having more than one language is an asset or a problem in aging is unclear. On the one hand, the language system is more complex, and there are more languages that use mental resources; on the other hand, the other languages may be useful as an additional path or tool. Recent work by Bialystok and her colleagues (Bialystok *et al.* 2004) suggests that cognitive functioning in later life may actually be affected by life-long experiences in handling two or more languages. Second language *learning* by elderly people has not been studied at all so far. This is remarkable since many multilingualism settings are settings in which migrants of different ages move to other countries where they have to deal with other languages. In many western-European countries there is now almost forced enculturation, including learning the national language for adult migrants irrespective of their age.

The structure of this book is as follows. In the first part we will discuss Dynamic Systems Theory briefly and show how it applies to language and language development. This leads us to a model of language and aging that appears to fit very well with general notions about development in general. We will discuss the state of the art with respect to language and aging from psycholinguistic and sociolinguistic perspectives. Historically, old age emerged as a distinct stage in life after the onset of industrialization when the continuous flow from adulthood to old age was institutionally disrupted by mandatory retirement. The notions of old age were reinforced by biomedicine which is one of the most powerful forces in framing notions about aging in contemporary society. Biomedicine, like psycholinguistics, tends to treat ageing as inherently problematic. Sociolinguistics tends to treat ageing as inherently unproblematic with the crisis in ageing being attributed to mediating factors like culture and language and the nature of the social cultural factors. The integrative approach we are adopting here tries to avoid the ageing as inherently problematic stance of psycholinguistics and the ageing as free from problems of sociolinguistics. The idea that ageing is inherently problematic is false positive, while the idea that ageing is free from problems is false negative. We will also discuss issues of language and dementia in multilingual settings. Both the assessment and treatment of dementia type disorders will be high on the agenda in many countries in the years to come, and few countries have made adequate provisions to take care of elderly multilinguals, both highly educated speakers of many foreign languages and lowly educated and illiterate speakers of many second languages in migrant settings. In the second part of the book we will discuss findings from ongoing studies on Afro-Americans, Hispanics and Chinese in the USA. Data from these projects will be related to the various theoretical notions discussed in the first part of the book.

Chapter 2

Language and Aging: A Dynamic Perspective

In this chapter we want to present a general framework by linking research on language and aging with ideas on the development of complex systems. We will first discuss some of the basic notions in Dynamic Systems Theory (DST) and then show how these may be applied to language development. DST is primarily a branch of mathematics concerned with abstract structures. For this a whole range of concepts and tools have been developed that now find applications in a wide range of disciplines – from marine biology to demographics and aerodynamics. DST was adopted readily by the sciences, but it took a while for cognitive science to make the link. In the last decade major steps have been made in many aspects of cognition such as visual perception, sensorimotor activity and more recently also language and language development (see Port & van Gelder, 1995 for an overview). Over the years DST has emerged as a new perspective on development of systems. Its full mathematical application is problematic in many areas of research, primarily because there is simply not enough information for the formulation of the complex mathematical equations DST is based on, but in many areas ideas based on DST have been applied successfully to describe and explain development without the full mathematical modeling.

The most simple definition of a dynamic system is: *a system of interacting variables that is constantly changing due to interaction with its environment and self reorganization*. In such a system the variables it consists of interact with each other. Other variables that do not interact with all these variables are not part of the system, though they will be part of a larger system in which subsystems are the variables that make up the system. Dynamic systems are constantly changing but development is not typically linear, it goes in leaps and bounds and it tends to settle in what are called attractor states. These are states the system converges to in preference over other possible states. The definition of 'environment' is very broad: it entails everything from the physical environment to the social environment, including peer groups, teaching and so on.

For the implementation of Dynamic systems, connectionist network models have been found to work best. In such models there are nodes and connections between them. As a result of activation of connections by input and output, such connections get stronger. When connections are not strengthened regularly, they deteriorate. One of the consequences of the use of connectionist models is that traditional ideas on storage and retrieval come under attack.

The starting point of Dynamic Systems Theory is that a developing system is maintained by a flux of energy. Every developing cognitive system is constrained by limited resources, such as memory, attention, motivation and other aspects. The system is in constant complex interaction with its environment and internal sources. Its multiple interacting components produce one or many self-organized equilibrium points, whose form and stability depend on the system's constraints. Growth is conceived of as an iterative process, which means that the present level of development depends critically on the previous level of development (van Geert, 1994).

Several researchers have looked at language as a dynamic system (van Geert 1994, 1998; Elman, 1995; Larsen-Freeman, 1997; Herdina & Jessner, 2002; de Bot *et al.*, 2005). A full treatment of all the ins and outs of this are well beyond the scope of the present book. Therefore the main aspects of the DST approach as far as they are relevant for this book can be summarized here:

- The aim of DST is to describe and explain development over time of complex systems.
- Systems consist of subsystems that interact.
- Changes in one of the subsystems have an impact on all other subsystems.
- Systems never completely settle as long as there are sufficient resources.
- Systems show variation over time.
- Systems develop through input from the environment and self-reorganization and have no in-built goal.
- Development can be growth or decline, and it is typically non-linear.
- Systems tend to settle temporarily in attractor states while they avoid other states, but when and how the system will settle cannot be predicted.
- Complexity emerges as a result of the interaction of variables, and the development of complex systems is unpredictable.
- Development is an iterative process: in each next step all the information of the previous steps is included.

The Application of DST in Cognition and Language Development

Language shows all the characteristics of a dynamic system, and accordingly language development can be viewed from a DST perspective: it is a system consisting of many subprocesses (e.g. pragmatic, syntactic, lexical, phonological) that interact (e.g. the syntactic and the pragmatic level), it shows variation over time, it develops through interaction and self-reorganization, it depends on internal and external resources, it shows growth and decline depending on the setting it is in, and it never settles completely. In development the system will temporarily settle in some states and not others (e.g. developmental stages in L1 and L2 development, fossilization as attractor states). Language use in the form of overt language production, but also subvocal use and inner speech probably play a role on the self-reorganization of the system: through use of elements in production, the position of those elements in the networks is strengthened. It could also be argued that output also acts as input for the system and that output in that way has an impact on the system.

Some aspects of language as a dynamic system are not generally accepted in linguistics: the idea that development has no goal but develops through incidental interactions between subsystems goes against ideas on universal grammar (UG) that argue that there is an in-built developmental path. Also the idea of continuing development goes against ideas of 'endstates' of development that are commonplace in UG thinking. The issue that places a DST approach to language in sharpest contrast with ideas on innateness is that complexity can develop through iteration (repeated application) of fairly simple operations. So the idea that complexity needs to be innate because it cannot come from input (the 'poverty of input' argument), does not hold.

The application of DST leads to a new approach to cognition and language. As Port and van Gelder argue in their introduction to *Mind as Motion. Exploration in the Dynamics of Cognition* (1995), the main problem is *time*. Most models of cognition and language processing, including such well-known models as the Levelt model for language production (1993), are steady state models, that is, models that try to capture the cognitive system as it is at a given moment in time. Development over time is presented as sequences of pictures of static states over time, like movies that suggest changes over time through rapid sequences of fixed pictures.

> Cognitive processes and their context unfold continuously and simultaneously in real time . . . The cognitive system is not a discrete sequential manipulator of static representational structures: rather, it

is a structure of mutually and simultaneously influencing change. Its processes do not take place in the arbitrary, discrete time of computer steps: rather, they unfold in the real time of ongoing change in the environment, the body, and the nervous system. The cognitive system does not interact with other aspects of the world by passing messages and commands: rather, it continuously coevolves with them. (Port & van Gelder, 1995: 3)

This means that static models lose their relevance and even their validity for the study development and that we have to look for other models that can deal with both the main findings on static systems and developing ones.

The Role of Resources in Language Development

For language development a distinction can be made between *internal resources*, resources within the developing individual: the capacity to develop, time to develop, internal informational resources such as conceptual knowledge and motivational resources, and *external resources*, resources outside the individual: spatial environments to explore, time invested by the environment to support development, external informational resources such as the language used by the environment, motivational resources such as reinforcement by the environment, and material resources. Memory capacity, perceptual and production skills, and aptitude to learn are all resources.

Resources in growth systems have two main characteristics: they are limited and they are interlinked in a dynamical system. The limitations hold for all internal resources: memory capacity is limited, as in the time available to spend on learning, the available knowledge and the amount of motivation to learn. The same goes for external resources: the variation of environments and their willingness to invest time and energy in learning support are limited as are the material resources. The fact that resources are limited has important consequences for language learning and language use: Van Geert (1994) argues that the development of the L1 lexicon shows leaps and bounds that can be related to changes outside the lexicon: e.g. the emergence of the multi-word sentence leads to a deceleration of the lexical growth in the one-word phase: while in the latter all resources could be used to develop the lexicon through the linking of different types of sensory information, in the next phase more resources are needed to develop the grammatical system needed for the functional distribution of information in multiple-word utterances. The resources must have some limited value for learning to take place: without memory, input or internal informational resources or motivation there will be no learning. At the same time there are compensatory relations between different types of resources: effort can compensate lack of time, motivation can compensate limited input from the environment. So resources are part of an interlinked dynamic structure. This holds for the interaction between internal and external resources as well: a growth in the child's informational resources will lead to a change in the interaction with the environment through a demand for more demanding tasks and environments. Also, a decline in language skills will lead to differences in language use with the environment and to a change of input.

The interlinked structure of resources is referred to as the 'cognitive ecosystem': 'each person has his or her own particular cognitive ecosystem consisting of internal as well as external or environment aspects' (van Geert 1994: 314). In DST terms, the resources define the state phase of the system. To give an example: the number of words an L2 learner has acquired is the resultant of the combined and interacting effects of the internal and external resources of time, input, motivation and attention.

Some Unresolved Issues: Attention and Intentionality

In research and models based on DST, it is obvious that DST has its roots in the hard sciences in which the agents looked at have complex but definable properties. When applying notions of DST in human cognition and language development, and learning and teaching, some issues come up that have not been dealt with adequately in DST models so far. The most obvious are the role of attention and intentionality. Weather systems and solar systems and even economic systems, which have figured prominently in the history of DST, are systems in which notions like attention and intentionality play no role. Such systems have no built-in direction they 'want' to go: they just develop. For human systems (and probably some animal systems) we have to deal with these other forces that are difficult to model but all important for behavior. It is not clear how in a dynamic system intentionality can be included, and how this variable in itself is related to other variables. In the list of internal resources for human learning we have simply included 'motivational resources' but in fact we know little about how that variable should be implemented. Something similar applies for various aspects of processing, but here the issues are slightly different: as indicated above, the addition of time as a variable has an enormous impact on the workings of processing models, as has the implementation along connectionist lines, which to a certain extent forces us to give up ideas on storage and retrieval in the traditional sense, while no real alternatives are available at the moment.

Language Development Across the Life Span

One of the most important outcomes of the DST approach is that language development as a process has no endpoint. If language is a dynamic system, it will continue to develop as long as the resources last. Most research has focused on the early stages of L1 and L2 development, and more on the growth side than on the decline side of development. There is a general tendency to view the end of puberty also as the end of L1 development. Language as a dynamic system, however, will continue to develop: there is constant interaction with the environment and the system is constantly reorganizing itself. There are many factors that may play a role in post-puberty language development: education, job requirements, relationships, parenthood and new hobbies are just a few of them. Different settings of language use will lead to differences in input and adaptations of the language system. While the differences in the first language in monolinguals may be relatively small (though no research has really looked at this so far in any detail), the acquisition and use of additional languages will have a major impact on the language system. Different languages can be viewed as subsystems within the larger language system (de Bot, 2004). The languages have an impact on each other. There is now substantial evidence that the first language, which for a long time was considered to be more or less immune to change after puberty, is influenced by the use of other languages (e.g. Kecsces & Papp, 2000; Dussias, 2001). Here, resources are the crucial issue. Following connectionist principles, linguistic elements as part of networks need to be used to be maintained. How much use is needed for maintenance we don't know, but research on migrants who have stopped using their mother tongue has shown that decline is the normal pattern (Schmid, 2003; Hulsen *et al.*, 2002). Apparently, not enough resources (in terms of amount of time of use) are invested or available to keep the language at the same level. While complete non-use is an obvious case for attrition, more subtle processes seem to be taking place in multilinguals: while monolinguals invest all their language-related resources to one language, multilinguals have to divide them over all their languages. Accordingly, the total of resources available has to be spread over these languages, and that will have an effect on the level of activation (as defined by speed of processing and retrievability of elements) of each language. This is also the gist of Grosjean's (1998) argument of the bilingual who is not two monolinguals in one person: the multilinguality changes the system and makes it different from a monolingual one. To what extent resources can be augmented for a specific task or subsystem and be taken from the resources for other systems is not clear.

Language development in aging

Apart from research on language attrition, research on non-pathological development in the age group between roughly speaking 18 and 55 is very scarce. There is some research on adult literacy development, but for spoken language the assumption seems to be that there is nothing of interest happening during that period. As the following chapters will show, there is considerable interest in language development in aging, with an emphasis on decline as the normal outcome. In the remainder of this chapter we want to show how a DST perspective on language development can be applied in an aging population.

When we go back to the basics of dynamic systems, three factors appear to be crucial for development: availability of resources, use of the language, and self-reorganization, though the latter factor is probably more a result of changes in the first two factors than a factor of its own. Because self-reorganization is not open to inspection, we will consider only availability of resources and use of the language as factors. So we could look at how changes in language proficiency are related to resources and use, but in the true DST spirit, it would be better to look at how language proficiency, language resources and language use interact. Each of these variables can be dissected into smaller variables that in themselves can be viewed as dynamic systems at a lower level. Also, like all other parts of the cognitive system, resources and language skills are both embodied and situated. This means that they function as part of a physical body, and changes in that physical system interact with cognitive variables. The situatedness of cognition means that characteristics of the setting also interact with the cognitive variables. Here the aging factor comes in: there are age-related physical changes that have an impact on cognitive functioning and accordingly language processing. But again, the relations are reciprocal: cognitive changes and changes in resources and language use have an impact on the physical system, as we hope to show later on. So we have a complex system with four interacting variables: the physical condition, the life setting, cognitive resources and language use. This system develops through the interaction of these variables. We will now discuss some of the core parameters of each of the variables.

Physical Changes

There is an enormous amount of research on various aspects of physical changes with aging on about every single subsystem in the body: the brains, the respiratory system, the metabolistic system, the muscular system, the blood system and so on. This is not a book on the physiology of aging, and we will not even try to summarize the main findings in the field.

We will simply have to accept that decline in various systems is given. Some changes have an impact on the cognitive system, in the sense that changes in the brain lead to a decline in memory capacity and speed of processing. But again this is not a one-way street. Cognitive changes may have an impact on physical aspects, e.g. when a lack of motivation to exercise leads to stiffening of the limbs and a loss of muscular strength.

The Life Setting

Under this heading we put different aspects of the how aging has an impact on how people live. Changes may be socio-psychological, such as the changes that come with retirement and an ensuing change of position in society, but also physical, such as a move to a retirement home. Also changes in the way people are looked at by their environment when they get older fall under this heading. Attitudes towards aging play a role in positioning elderly people in society. This also relates to self-perceptions of what it means to be old and the elderlies' attitudes towards the changing environment. The life setting in itself is a dynamic system because social and physical changes interact with perceptions of the outside world and perceptions and attitudes from that outside world. Again, rather than seeing old age as a stage, aging is about a system in development. Interactions with the outside world and changes in those interactions are at least as important in this process as the internal changes within the individual. In Chapter 3 we will discuss a number of aspects of the life setting that relate to language:

- attitudes towards the elderly and aging;
- changes in communication patterns within and between generations;
- the use of special registers ('elderspeak') with elderly people.

Cognitive Resources

The cognitive system consists of a number of subsystems that all play a role in language use and language development. Whether there is something like a separate language system is one of the issues that have emerged from research in DST (Thelen & Smith, 1994), but for the moment we will assume that the language system can be decomposed into a number of subcomponents. These subcomponents interact with relevant subsystems including memory, attention, perception and speech-related motor skills. In Chapter 5 we will discuss relevant findings on cognitive resources that relate to language:

- working memory capacity and long-term memory capacity;
- attentional processes;
- speed of processing.

Language Skills and Language Use

Though language is clearly part of the cognitive system and can be seen as a cognitive resource, we will discuss it separately here. In research on language and aging, language skills are typically taken as the dependent variable: the aim is to find out what the impact of other types of changes is on language skills. As will be obvious by now, a dynamic approach to language development implies that the language system is in interaction with other systems and that linguistic changes have an impact on other systems. As indicated earlier, language production has an impact on the internal structure of the language system: use leads to change, but it also has an impact on other systems. We will argue that language use has an impact on the life setting, and on cognitive resources.

Under this heading we also discuss bilingualism and multilingualism as a factor. While the overwhelming majority of studies on language and aging take a monolingual perspective, there is now a growing awareness that more than half of the world's population is in fact bilingual or multilingual. From the by now vast amount of research on language use and linguistic skills in the elderly we will look at the following aspects in Chapter 4:

- Language production
  - at the pragmatic level;
  - at the lexical level;
  - at the morpho-syntactic level;
  - at the phonological level.

- Language perception
  - at the pragmatic level;
  - at the lexical level;
  - at the morpho-syntactic level;
  - at the phonological level.

- Bilingualism and multilingualism

Bringing Together Different Strands in Research on Language and Aging

The aim of this chapter is to present a general framework on development and show how language and aging fits in that framework. In addition we want to use the framework to organize and interpret the research on language and aging. In chapter 3 the state of the art is presented along sociolinguistic lines, which coincides with the variables under life setting above. In Chapter 4 we focus on research from a psycholinguistic perspective, which includes the variables listed above under cognitive resources and language skills and use. These two lines represent different worlds and different research communities with only few researchers (Kemper, Ryan) contributing to both. In our view there is good reason to bring these two lines together because the two perspectives are complementary rather than competing. In the conclusion of her overview on language and aging, Kemper concludes that:

> . . . a negative spiral can result in which age-related language impairments plus negative stereotyping lead to the ascription of incompetence and dependency to older adults, patronizing speech, and limited opportunities for social interaction: as a result, older adults may become socially withdrawn or depressed and suffer a further erosion of language skills. (Kemper *et al.*, 1995: 540).

Ryan's 'Communicative Predicament of Aging' model is based on the same kind of reasoning: language changes and age stereotypes interact, leading to a change of interaction with and by elderly people which in turn has an impact on language skills. In this chapter we want to develop this line of reasoning further by adding a psycholinguistic perspective to the explanation of decline of language with age. The main argument we want to push is that language use, input and output, are crucial for maintaining language skills, and that the changes in communicative behavior pointed out by Kemper and Ryan lead to a decline of quality of language use. In the model we present, the focus is on the interaction between language skills, language use, memory and mental processing on the one hand, and the use of elderspeak and low quality interaction with elderly people on the other.

Pathological and Non-pathological Aging

In the literature on cognitive functioning of elderly people, one of the issues is, to what extent decline in different types of dementia should be seen as a fundamentally different process, or rather as a more dense version of normal development. From a DST perspective, there is no principled difference between the two processes: the same mechanisms of interacting systems apply; also when the pace of development in one system changes, e.g. due to a change in memory capacity or speed of processing which reflect changes in the brain. As indicated above, development depends on resources and a growth point. When one of the crucial resources decline to the point that they basically break down, development in a part of the system will come to a stop. It could be argued that in advanced dementia several of the core resources no longer function, maybe because supply is short, maybe because the interaction between systems has stopped. Even in very advanced dementia, the system is developing, but the development is mainly the decline of resources and the fading away of links between systems.

In this chapter issues of language and aging are discussed within a Dynamic Systems Theory (DST) perspective. In this perspective, which focuses on the change over time of complex systems, languages, like all other dynamic systems, are constantly changing due to interactions with other systems and due to internal reorganization. This leads to a life-span perspective which is well suited to explain language change in aging. It is argued here that due to changes in resources for language use, such as memory, perception and attention, language skills change, but at the same time the changes in the language system have an impact on other systems, both within the individual and in its environment. Language change in aging is seen as the interaction between internal changes due to physical changes in the organism and external changes that have to do with perceptions of aging in society at large and elderly people's reactions to this. Rather than seeing social aspects of aging and decline as separated from physical and psychological changes, we argue that there is a dynamic interaction between the changes at different levels which calls for an integrative approach to the study of language and aging.

Chapter 3

Language and Communication with the Elderly

In this chapter we want to look at the language used by and among elderly people from a sociolinguistic perspective. Language is one of the aspects of the life setting of elderly people because language is the main means of communication for most people. Language also reflects many aspects of the life setting: with whom do elderly people talk, what do they talk about, how do they talk and how are they talked to. There is a considerable body of research on language used in interaction with and by elderly people. One line of research looks at various aspects of the way the elderly are spoken to. Three aspects of the discussion on 'elderspeak' as it is generally called, are relevant here. The first is, what are the characteristics of the language used in communication with elderly people; the second, to what extent accommodation to perceived communicative problems of elderly people actually helps to make communication more effective; and the third, to what extent are such adaptations of speech valued by the elderly interactants. The second line of research (which partly overlaps with the first) is on the evaluation of the way elderly people speak. We will discuss the literature on these two lines. First we want to place the study of language and aging in a broader perspective.

Elderspeak, Stereotypes and Ageism

There are two sides of the elderspeak discussion. One is how it affects meaningful interactions in a positive or negative way and the psycholinguistic effects this has on language skills. The other is to what extent and how elderspeak reflects and defines aging in society. In addition, to what extent do elderly people go along with such definitions. This is part of the broader discussion on the role of language in defining aging. Coupland (1997) presents a review of research on the relation of language and aging from a sociolinguistic and socio-psychological perspective. His main thesis is that ageism, that is, the portraying of aging as a process of inevitable decline, is to a large extent defined by language used by both the elderly and the non-elderly population. Studying the language used in relation to aging has allowed us '. . . to begin to capture how language mediates perceptions of the lifespan, how inter-generational talk can be organized interactively, how life-developmental rituals are marked and achieved linguistically, how people's personal identities are discursively negotiated, and how criteria of age-appropriateness are invoked in a host of communicative settings' (p. 27). In his analysis Coupland uses Tajfel's inter-group theory which argues that group membership is not fixed but negotiated and partly self-defined. It also stresses that individuals are by definition members of various social groups. Having a certain age is only one of many definitions of identity and again not a fixed one. In defining groups, social stereotypes play an important role and they define boundaries between social groups, but some boundaries are more permeable than others. Stereotypes define interactions between groups to a large extent, and for aging the interaction between and with elderly people as a social group tends to be dominated by beliefs with respect to decline. In a number of studies Giles and his colleagues (Giles *et al.*, 2002; McCann *et al.*, 2005) have looked at beliefs about intergenerational communication. In their work, they focus on young adults' perception of age stereotypes of young adults, middle-aged adults and elderly adults. The constant finding is that older adults are perceived as more benevolent, but less vital and these perceptions define reported interest in communicating with elderly. For both factors the middle-aged adult group take a position between the younger and the older group. In a follow-up study with undergraduate students in the United States, South Africa and Ghana, Giles and Makoni (2004) found that perceptions of age stereotypes were largely similar between those groups. An interesting finding in this study was that the definition in age of age groups showed significant differences between cultural groups. While elderly age begins at around 60 for the American students, this is about 50 for the South African and Ghanese students.

Interestingly, ethnographic data on interaction between doctors and elderly patients show that the stereotype of decline is endorsed by the elderly themselves and that it is their doctors who try to change that stereotype by redefining physical malfunctioning from age-related (and therefore irreversible) decline to a curable temporary symptom (referred to in Coupland 1997).

In the American literature on aging two types of elderly people are often distinguished: the 'Despondent' elderly and the 'Golden Ager'. For elderly people these two types appear to have differential effects on ways they are spoken to. Hummert *et al.* (1998) had younger and older adults rate the type of style they would use to these two types of elderly people in a hospital context and in a community context. There was a tendency towards more patronizing speech towards the despondent type and in the hospital context. In particular the preference for patronizing speech with the Golden Agers increased significantly in the hospital setting compared to the community setting. Older subjects were less inclined to use patronizing messages than younger subjects. In an earlier study Hummert *et al.* (1994) presented a similar picture of what they then called 'The perfect grandparent', someone who is lively, sociable, interesting and well-informed as opposed to the complaining, bitter and prejudiced 'shrewd/curmudgeon'. Studies like this make it clear that treating all individuals aged 70 or older as one single and monolithic group in terms of behavior or stereotyping is unwarranted. Still, many studies do exactly that. As Orange and Ryan (2000) indicate, individuals' profiles in communication may differ dramatically and in particular in interaction with elderly people, and care takers have to be aware of the fact that communication is not just exchange of information but is also about care, mutual respect and the patients' self-identity and autonomy.

Characteristics of Elderspeak

What causes the use of elderspeak?

The interest in characteristics of the language used in communication with elderly people started in the early 1980s (e.g. Ashburn & Gordon, 1981; Ramig, 1986; Cohen & Faulkner, 1986). One of the questions was, what caused speakers to use elderspeak. De Wilde and de Bot (1989) did a study to find out whether professional care takers adapt their style of language use to the perceived degree of decline of the elderly interactants. The interactions with 10 elderly people in a home for the elderly were analyzed with respect to different aspects of elderspeak. Five of the informants had a high score on the Short Portable Mental Status Questionnaire (SPMSQ) and five with a low score. The two groups differed significantly in terms of cognitive decline and dependence of care. The outcomes show that significantly more elderspeak is used with the informants with a low score on the SPMSQ, so degree of alertness is a predictor of the use of elderspeak. These findings are in line with other findings in the literature on elderspeak (Caporael & Culbertson, 1983; Ryan, Hummert and Boich 1995).

The effects of elderspeak

A substantial number of experiments have been carried out to evaluate the effects of various types of elderspeak. Kemper and her colleagues (Kemper *et al.*, 1995; Kemper & Harden, 1999) looked at positive and

negative aspects of elderspeak. In their experiments a referential communication task was used in which listeners were required to trace a route on a
map on the basis of information from a video-recorded speaker. Various
aspects of the speech were manipulated to test the effectiveness of the conveyance of the information. The listeners' route was compared to the target
route and deviations were used as on-line quantitative measures of comprehension. In addition the listeners were asked to self-report on the
success of the communication and to evaluate the speaker. The outcomes
show that:

> providing semantic elaborations and reducing the use of subordinate
> and embedded clauses benefit older adults and improve their perfor-
> mance on the referential communication task, whereas reducing
> sentence length, slowing speaking rate and using high pitch do not.
> The use of short sentences, a slow rate of speaking, and high pitch
> resulted in the older adults' reporting more communication problems.
> (Kemper & Harden, 1999: 656)

One of the negative effects of the use of elderspeak is that it may have a
detrimental effect on the self-esteem of elderly people. This is what Ellen
Ryan and her colleagues at McMaster University have called the 'Communicative Predicament of Aging' model. This model is based on the
assumption that the kind of modifications in speech referred to as
elderspeak are 'primarily based on negative expectations of incompetence
and dependency that occur independently of actual functioning' (Ryan *et
al.* 2000: 272). Such modifications limit the possibilities of meaningful interaction and reinforce age-related stereotyping. Repeated exposure to it may
lead to reduced self-esteem and withdrawal, which leads to further expectations of incompetence and so on to a negative feedback loop. The risk of
such a negative spiral is greater in nursing homes where residents are more
dependent on staff, and where negative stereotypes may be present. In
their 2000 study, Ryan *et al.* looked at the effects of residents' reactions to
patronizing speech from a nurse and the evaluation of the nurses' accommodation and non-accommodation following these reactions.
Interestingly, the continuation of the patronizing style was devalued by all
informants (community seniors, residents and nursing home staff), but
residents seem to accept it more easily, reporting that this is the way communication goes in that setting. Evidence for setting-specific evaluations of
a patronizing speech style also comes from work by Hummert and Mazloff
(2001). They studied perceptions of and responses to patronizing advice in
two contexts: in hospital and in the community. A patronizing advice style
appeared to be accepted as legitimate in the hospital setting but not in the
community setting.

As mentioned earlier, elderspeak appears to be used in particular with elderly people who show signs of cognitive decline and there seems to be a natural tendency in speakers to adapt their way of speaking based on perceived communication problems. Kemper *et al.* (1994) looked at the speech register used by spouses when interacting with adults showing such decline. The speech produced by both groups was analyzed with respect to syntactic complexity (MLU, mean number of clauses per utterance), use of personal and indefinite pronouns, main verbs, conjunctions, negation, types of question, semantic complexity (propositional density) and content of the description. The picture descriptions of the two groups differed in a number of respects. The AD patients were syntactically correct but semantically and content-wise disorganized and vague compared to the spouses' descriptions. As in other studies syntax seemed to be remarkably well retained. The patients' MLU exceeded that of the spouses', but the sentences were semantically empty and redundant. In their speech towards the patients, the spouses reduced the syntactical complexity and the propositional density and restricted their descriptions to highly frequent and highly salient elements in the pictures. The correct scores of the patients showed that these accommodations were successful. Apparently the spouses were aware of the specific problems of their partners. The accommodations appeared to have a positive effect on the demented patients' subsequent description of the pictures. Similar positive effects are reported by Gould *et al.* (2002), who presented younger and older adults with medical instruction on tape in either neutral speech or elderspeak. The older adults showed better recall of the instructions and were also more positive about the use of elderspeak.

An intriguing question following from this finding is, to what extent effective elderspeak can be taught in order to improve communication. Williams *et al.* (2003) report on a study in which nurses in five nursing homes received training to make them aware of the use of elderspeak and to foster the use of effective communication strategies in interactions with residents. In a pre-test-treatment-post-test setting they showed that the intervention led to a reduction of the use of elderspeak and to the use of a register that is less controlling and more respectful.

The evaluation of elderspeak

As mentioned in the introduction, the third line of research on elderspeak deals with the evaluation of elderspeak by the elderly themselves. In some of the research discussed above evaluations were part of the study. Elderspeak has this Janus' head characteristic of being at the same time a sign of care and a sign of lack of respect. Ryan *et al.* (1994) tried to isolate the evaluation of the patronizing part of elderspeak from the nurturing quality of the communication. Interestingly they found that care takers who use elderspeak are rated as being less respectful and competent, but not as less nurturing.

One aspect that has so far attracted little attention is to what extent there are cultural differences with respect to the use and evaluation of elderspeak. Sachweh (1998) reports on a study on the use of elderspeak in a German nursing home. It was found that German nurses did use elderspeak (or Secondary Babytalk as they called it), but that the residents did not necessarily react negatively: some elderly people actually reacted extremely positively. To what extent this reflects cultural differences between American and German culture along the lines of Hofstede's (2001) model of cultural values is not clear but certainly worth pursuing.

Most of the work on elderspeak has been carried out in institutional settings. That is in itself already a very specific situation that is typical of societies in which elderly people are defined and treated as a special group, and no longer as an integral part of society. There is also quite some work on medical interaction with the elderly (see Coupland _et al._, 1991 for an overview), but while this may not be formally communication in an institutional setting, it is still a very specific setting. Research on non-institutional settings is missing, and it would be particularly interesting to see how interaction with the elderly takes place in different cultures, and to what extent this register is also used in non-institutionalized settings, whether young children also use elderspeak, and whether elderly people among themselves use such a register. There is ample evidence for the use of specific registers with elderly people, but in many societies and culture, this register is based on respect rather than perceived decline.

Evaluations of the Way Elderly People Speak

The way elderly people speak is part of how they present themselves. To what extent ways of speaking are part of more or less conscious self-defining behavior or simply the result of physiological and cognitive changes and not open to conscious control is unclear, and quite likely the two mechanisms interact. In the previous sections some of the literature on how younger generations interact with elderly people has been discussed. The general finding was that elderspeak is often valued negatively by both young and old. Interestingly the use of elderspeak, or maybe we should say the wrong type of elderspeak, leads to negative evaluations of both the care taker and the elderly that are spoken to in a patronizing way. La Tourette and Meeks (2000) refer to this as the 'blame the victim' effect in communication with the elderly. Clearly this double negative effect makes a critical view and use of elderspeak all the more necessary. On what language characteristics younger generations classify individuals as old and how they value that (and accordingly how that influences their own behavior towards elderly people) is not really clear. Bieman-Copland and Ryan (2001) looked at the effects of repetitive language on age-related perceptions of young and young-old (mean age 67 years) listeners. Both groups valued the repetitious language use negatively since it seems to reflect an inability to monitor the conversation and is therefore seen as a sign of cognitive decline. In an earlier study the same authors had shown that memory successes are seen as less typical for older than for younger speakers (Bieman-Copland & Ryan, 1998).

As will be discussed in Chapter 4, there are clear age effects on the phonological level: there is a strong correlation between specific voice characteristics and age. Hummert *et al.* (1999) looked at the role of voice characteristics in age stereotypes. Young listeners appeared to be accurate in assessing the age of elderly in the 60–69, 70–79 and 80 and over age groups. For elderly males, vocal volume was the best indicator of age, while for elderly females voice pitch and vocal jitter were positively related to age.

Communication Within and Between Generations

Not all communication with elderly people can be placed under the elderspeak label. It is quite likely that in most conversations with elderly people younger people do adapt their style of communication, but not in a way different from what they would do with any other individual. Accommodation is a normal part of interaction. Language use only becomes elderspeak when it shows the characteristics mentioned earlier. Satisfaction with intra- and intergenerational communication was studied by Chen and King (2002). Not surprisingly communication satisfaction was higher in interaction between participants that had positive stereotypes towards the other age group than when stereotypes were neutral or negative. Overall, the old adults expressed less satisfaction in communication than the younger group, irrespective of the age of the individual they interacted with.

Age-related stereotypes also play a role in everyday communication means like the telephone. As Ryan *et al.* (2003) show, young adults expect elderly people to have more problems in the use of the telephone, even though elderly people's self-reports are less negative. It is quite likely that hearing loss and the need to 'hurry up' on the telephone has a negative impact, also because contextual cues are absent, making communication less redundant.

Critical Approaches to Language-based Approaches in Healthcare

In line with the work by Coupland discussed in the first section of this chapter, critical approaches based on discourse analysis and deconstructionist views have come up. McGowan *et al.* (2000) looked at the way in which managers in healthcare talk about aging and care, and showed how covert perceptions of what constitutes 'old' and 'care' play a role in the perspectives on eldercare.

Another approach is discussed by Vittoria (1999) who describes the process of development of a socially constructive view on dementia in which the perceptions of the patients are validated. 'In this "different" world, as the [nursing assistants] call the world of the Unit, the resident is depicted as a socially responsive actor with a surviving self that is to be treated with respect.' (p. 361). In such an approach the balance between comforting and demeaning behavior in communication is probably easier to strike than in settings in which the 'different world' is basically denied and the characteristics of the elderly interactants devalued.

Communication with Elderly People in Multilingual Nursing Homes

In many Western societies people with a migrant background are either residents or staff in nursing homes. Such homes are becoming more and more multilingual and multicultural in recent years. While most of the residents acquired levels of proficiency of the local language to do their job and carry out everyday communication in it, there is a tendency in elderly migrants to retreat in their own cultural and linguistic community. Even migrants who tended not to live together when they arrived and when they were younger, prefer to spend the later years among people with a similar background, sharing memories and cultural values from the past (Clyne, 1977; Overberg, 1984). There is also a tendency to revert to the mother tongue in old age. This is likely to be the result of a decline in use of the second language in the setting in which the mother tongue is used more widely, and for groups with lower levels of education it reflects limited skills in the second language to start with. De Bot and Clyne (1989) looked at language skills in elderly Dutch migrants in Australia and found language reversion for those migrants who didn't acquire high levels of proficiency in English. In-depth interviews with some of the participants made it clear that in particular the women, who typically stayed at home to take care of the children and the household, learned only very basic survival English and may not have reached the threshold that in other studies has been shown to lead to retention of language skills (Weltens, 1989; Murtagh, 2003).

This tendency to return to the mother tongue as the preferred language of communication poses serious problems in nursing homes. Residents with different mother tongues will have little opportunity to interact in their preferred language. Few people move into nursing home when they retire. The normal pattern is that after retirement contacts with old friends from the home country are picked up again and friendships within the ethnic group become more important. With that comes the increased use of the mother tongue or quite often a mixed variety of the mother tongue and the local language. Only when serious health problems develop will those people move into nursing homes. By that time they are likely to feel more comfortable among their 'own people' and speaking their own language. In nursing homes that will become a problem, because numbers are often too small locally to set up nursing homes for specific ethnic groups. Severe communication problems and related social isolation will typically occur in such settings. For groups that are large enough and have sufficient financial means, nursing homes have been set up that take care of their own people, often bringing in doctors and nurses from the home country (e.g. the Dutch in Australia, Overberg, 1985; see also Chapter 8 on Chinese elderly in the USA).

In fact the picture is even more complicated. Elderly people with a migrant background may end up in a nursing home in which the majority of the residents and staff speak a different language, for instance a Moroccan man in a monolingual French nursing home. Another possibility is a multi-ethnic/multilingual nursing home in which residents with different mother tongues live together with staff that speak only the local language. A third option that emerges more and more in western Europe is that speakers of the local languages find themselves in a nursing home in which a part of the staff are actually not speakers of that local language. In countries like the Netherlands first and second generation migrants have a career in the nursing profession. There have even been actions to attract nurses from countries like the Philippines to cater for the increasing need for nurses. This latter type of setting may also lead to communication problems between residents and staff (as one of the authors has experienced with his mother). As we will see in Chapter 4, good quality interaction may be vital for the maintenance or slowing down of decline of linguistic skills in the elderly. A setting in which the quality of the language is degraded is a hazard in this respect. This is not meant to devalue the important role of migrant nurses. Many of them come from cultures in which respect for old age is very important and the quality of their care and dedication compensates well what they may lack in language skills.

Summary

In this chapter we have discussed only a part of the large body of research on communication with and among elderly people. To summarize what we know about the effects of elderspeak, it is clear that depending on how alert they are perceived, elderly people are often spoken to in a specific way. There appear to be two motives for the use of such a register: to overcome communication problems, that is, to improve the transmission of information, and to express care and concern, that is to enhance personal relations. The use of elderspeak can have various effects. Positive effects are that communication is indeed improved when semantic elaborations are provided and complex sentence structures are avoided. Other characteristics of comparable registers, such as baby-talk and foreigner talk, short sentences, exaggerated intonation and a very slow speaking rate appear to have a negative effect both in terms of the transmission of information and affectively. A patronizing or condescending style is generally devalued both by the elderly themselves and by members of staff in nursing homes, but the acceptance of such registers appears to be influenced by the settings in which they are used. In hospital settings and for institutionalized elderly such a style seems to be more acceptable than in other settings and for community elderly. A remarkable finding is that in experimental settings, elderly people when coupled in dyads with other elderly people or younger people, show little variation in their speaking style. Elderspeak is a style typically used by younger speakers, not by elderly speakers, unless they are talking to other elderly people who show signs of cognitive decline. The right type of elderspeak, affective but not too patronizing, avoiding semantic and syntactic complexity, is both effective in improving comprehension and is valued positively by elderly people. The wrong type of elderspeak, condescending, and more baby-talk like with a low speech rate and exaggerated intonation and over-short and choppy sentences is detrimental to communication, is devalued and leads to a decline in self-respect in elderly people. Continued use of such a style of speaking may have very negative effects.

Language appears to play an important role of the elderly as a social group, both through external definition and through self-description. Stereotypes based on an association of aging with decline are still dominant, though the recent 'discovery' of the Golden Ager appears to be a trend that looks more at the positive aspects of aging. At the same time it could be argued that this is a subtle way to victimize those who do not have the fortune to age in such a way, not unlikely due to lower levels of education and income over the life span.

A fairly new trend in research on aging is geared towards elderly in multilingual settings, in particular for elderly in nursing homes in which their preferred language may not be spoken to them, either because no one speaks it, or because staff and residents speak different languages. We will come back to this in Chapter 5 in which we will discuss language and aging in multilingual settings.

How does this relate to the ideas on language and aging based on DST? As indicated in Chapter 2, the individual's language system can be seen as a dynamic system in interaction with other dynamic systems. Changes in the individual such as decline in alertness, or the emergence of age-specific speech characteristics lead to changes in the other systems: the individual is seen as less capable and the style of interacting is adapted accordingly. Here the dynamic aspect becomes clearly visible: the change in style of interacting will in turn have an effect on the elderly individual who may suffer a decline in self-esteem and withdraw from communicating altogether. Multilingualism, and in particular the absence of a language shared by care giver and care taker, may lead to even more dramatic changes. In the last chapter we will take these issues up again and see how changes in language skills and the availability of resources interact with changes in the life setting and more in particular in communication patterns.

Chapter 4

Language Use and Language Skills in Healthy and Pathological Aging

In this chapter the findings on language proficiency in the elderly will be discussed. In the previous chapters we have argued for a DST perspective on language and aging, which means that we have to look at both language-related resources and language skills as such. There is not a long tradition of research in this topic. The increased interest in language and dementia has stimulated a parallel interest in language in non-demented age-matched populations, at first to provide healthy control data for the disordered group, but gradually developing into a subfield of its own. For most of the aphasia-tests available age-related norms have been developed, but exactly why and on the basis of what such norms have been generated is not clear, in particular in light of the view on aging that considers age as an index variable rather than an explanatory variable. We will present data on language production and language perception at the phonological, lexical, syntactical and pragmatic level separately for healthy and pathological aging.

Some Methodological Issues in Research on Language and Aging

One of the main problems is that it is not always exactly clear what 'linguistic skills' have been studied and what that means for language use: e.g. there is quite some research on hearing loss, but it is not always clear to what extent pure tone loss leads to problems in hearing normal speech in conversation. Similarly, a decline in the ability to retrieve words from memory in laboratory settings and experiments may not tell us that much about the impact of word findings problems in normal interaction. In addition, both the number of informants and the types of test used may not be ideal for this kind of study. It could be claimed that the methodology used is more suitable for the finding decline than for finding retention or changes that are not necessarily in decline. In most studies, a group of elderly informants is compared with a group of younger informants without taking into account possible cohort effects, which may play a decisive role, especially since there is a correlation between age and level of education in most Western countries (cf. Kynette & Kemper, 1986: 66).

Another contentious issue is the selection of informants in this type of research. Hamilton (1999) suggests two options in research of this type: very large-scale studies that allow for generalization to the whole population, or case studies and small-scale studies. A problem with the large-scale studies that Hamilton herself mentions is the increasing diversity over the life span. Rather than becoming more _similar_ with increasing age, people become more _diverse_ over time, which makes it very difficult to include all that variation in one study or sample. There are obvious advantages of the case study approach, but the generalizability of the findings remains a problem, again in light of the diversity within the group. In most psycholinguistic research, random selection of informants is the normal procedure. In fact, most statistics are based on the equiprobability assumption: every member and accordingly every characteristic of a population has an equal probability of being included in the sample. Schaie (1977: 53) questions the desirability of such an approach for research on cognitive functioning in the elderly:

> Because of the severe problems in maintaining the representative characteristics of any panel in the design and the logistic problems involved in controls for experimental mortality, most investigators should ask themselves whether they are in fact interested in estimating population parameters. Perhaps the major purpose of their research question is to study how a given behavior is expressed at different developmental stages under conditions which may be idealized or extreme.

He concludes that a strong argument can be made for gathering data under optimal intellectual conditions in old age and suggests that it might be useful to work with samples of the active, well functioning and intelligent aged.

An example of such a study is the one by Lintsen and de Bot (1989) who studied the relation between language proficiency and education in a group of still independently living, fairly highly educated individuals aged between 65 and 89 years. A large set of tests was used and the analyses show that for this particular group there were age-related effects of memory decline (as evidenced by data from verbal fluency and digit span tasks) and perceptual decline (as evidenced by data from phoneme discrimination and repetition tasks). No age-related effects were found for semantic and syntactic processing. Incidentally, the data from that project show how much the different subsystems (memory, perception, language) interact: in the factor analyses memory and perception tasks also showed loadings on the language factor and conversely, linguistic tests showed loadings on the memory and perception factors.

The last finding brings us to another problem in research on language and aging: the setting apart of language as a separate skill or module. Due to the immense impact of structuralist and later Chomskian linguistics, language has become more and more retracted from other parts of the cognitive system. While recent neuro-imaging research has shown that there are indeed parts of the brain that play a crucial role in language processing, there is also evidence that other parts of the brain are involved and that the so-called language areas are also active in other tasks (Stowe & Haverkort, 2003). In the DST approach advocated here, there may be methodological arguments to set linguistics skills apart from other cognitive skills, but the 'total interconnectedness' of dynamic systems also applies to language: there is no language without memory (and the other way around some would argue) and language does not emerge as a separate faculty. This is probably the one message we want to convey in this book: a focus on language as a separate skill or commodity distorts the picture of what language in use means. This is in line with earlier suggestions that non-linguistic aspects of language use, such as peripheral perception and memory capacity, may play a role in language decline with age. In the discussion of their large cross-sequential study on language and aging, Obler and Albert (1989: 11) conclude: 'We have recently become convinced that the language changes of aging are related to non-language cognitive changes more deeply than we had thought.'

In this chapter we will discuss the general trends by focusing on language production and language perception and the role of memory, education, perception and linguistic knowledge in language processing in both healthy and cognitively impaired elderly people. We will discuss language perception and language production separately as far as possible, but in many tasks used (e.g. various repetition tasks) the two cannot be easily distinguished.

Language Production

Phonological Aspects and speech characteristics

Voice characteristics of elderly people change: pitch goes up, there is more jitter and in particular due to changes in the vocal tract (such as dentures) articulation deteriorates (Linville & Rens, 2001). De Leeuw and Mahieu (2004) report on a longitudinal study of vocal aging and show that there is a significant deterioration of the acoustic voice signal and increased vocal roughness. Self-reported voice instability leads to changes in social life, such as avoiding social gatherings. As indicated in Chapter 3, elderly voices change so much that estimation of age on the basis of voice characteristics is fairly accurate. One of the characteristics that show subtle but effective changes is voice onset time (VOT). Larson *et al.* (1992) present VOT data from three age groups (25–39 years, 60–69 years and 70–79 years). Results show that there were significant differences in VOT for /p/ and /t/ in the older speakers.

Normal fluency in speech seems to be only mildly affected in aging. Studies on the role of age in normal spoken conversations show only slightly higher disfluency rates for older speakers as compared to young and middle-aged speakers (Bortfeld *et al.* 2001). There is a tendency for the elderly group to show more disfluencies such as hesitations and filled pauses when the topic discussed is more complex and abstract, which may point to problems in planning speech and a reduction of resources for speaking (Kemper, 1992).

Lexical aspects

Picture naming is probably the most widely used task for assessing production problems in aging. Au *et al.* (1995) conducted a seven-year longitudinal study with normal subjects aged 30–79. Naming performance showed a significant decline over time, in particular for the older groups. They conclude that the decline in naming ability is more than a breakdown in lexical retrieval but also reflects changes in perceptual and semantic processing. A further refinement of the naming paradigm was used by Barresi *et al.* (2000) in order to disentangle the effects of impaired access and semantic degradation as explanations for lower naming scores. In all age groups (50s, 60s and 70s) more naming failures could be attributed to impaired access than to semantic degradation. Some more semantic degradation effects were found for the 70s group. Similar findings have been reported by Hodgson and Ellis (1998). Schmitter-Edgecombe *et al.* (2000) compared three age groups: young adults, young-old adults and old-old adults, in a confrontational naming task and a more discourse based vocabulary task and found that the older adults groups made more word retrieval errors, but these groups showed higher naming accuracy than the young adults group. They conclude that tests of discourse may be better measures, in the sense of more valid, but also more sensitive, for assessing everyday word-finding difficulties in healthy older adults. They make the observation that old-old adults may have learned to compensate for word-retrieval problems in spontaneous discourse by not initiating responses or avoiding items that might produce difficulty (p. 489).

Another widely used language production measure is the verbal fluency test. In this test, subjects have to give as many words as they can within a given amount of time (one or two minutes) of a specific category. Phonological verbal fluency (words beginning with a specific letter or sound) and semantic verbal fluency (words from categories like fruits, furniture, boys' names) are the most widely used versions of the test. The verbal fluency test is considered to be a good instrument to assess word-finding problems, but it also tests working memory capacity because words have to be stored during the test in order to avoid repetition of the same word. The test is part of practically all tests of aphasia, and there is an enormous set of data on this for different types of language disorders. Aphasia tests have also been used widely to assess language performance in elderly and demented adults. Kempler _et al._ (1998) provide an overview of findings in a study on the effects of age, education and ethnicity on verbal fluency. They had a group of 317 healthy subjects between 54 and 99 years of age from different cultural and linguistic backgrounds perform an animal naming task in their first language. There were clear differences between ethnic groups in the animals named. This will be discussed in more detail in Chapter 5. Fluency scores were higher for younger subjects and for subjects with higher levels of education.

Related to findings on word/picture naming and verbal fluency is research in the Tip-of-the-Tongue (TOT) phenomenon. Heine _et al._ (1999) compared young adults with a group of young-olds (60–74) and old-olds (80–92) in experimentally induced TOT states: the informants had to produce a word on the basis of a definition of the targets to be retrieved. The three age groups appeared to differ on both the rate of occurrence of TOT experiences and the time needed to solve them. Interestingly, given enough time even the oldest group managed to solve the TOT states, which suggest that the lexical knowledge is largely there, but more difficult to retrieve. Word-finding problems manifest themselves in different forms: circumlocution, empty speech, and pauses may actually be caused by word-finding problems and strategies to compensate for that. The locus of the retrieval problems does not seem to lie in the connection between concepts and lemmas, but rather between lemmas and lexemes, i.e. the word form (Burke _et al._, 1991). While the impact of education on findings with regard to naming has been studied in some detail, many other factors that could play a role have not. Goulet _et al._ (1994) reviewed 25 earlier studies on naming in the elderly and found no consistent picture. In their view a large number of what they call 'nuisance factors', which include education, health status and medication, have not been taken care of sufficiently to support the claim made in many studies that naming ability declines with aging.

Syntactic aspects

With respect to syntax, there are again effects of reduced working memory capacity, leading to a preference for more simplified syntax (such as right-branching over left-branching sentences), but in undemanding settings older adults appear to be able to use complex syntax without problems. As in most of the literature on language in the elderly, the definition of 'syntax' is not always clear in Kemper's work. While various aspects of syntax have been tested, it remains unclear how lexical, semantic and stylistic aspects are separated from 'pure' syntax. As indicated for the Lintsen and de Bot (1989) study it is difficult to separate the effects at the syntactical level from effects on other levels, in particular when memory load is taxed. Kemper (1992) shows that elderly people are less likely to start difficult sentences, probably because the memory load for producing such sentences is too high. In their research on aging and the loss of grammatical forms, Kynette and Kemper (1986) present data on spontaneous speech. Again elderly informants avoid grammatical forms and syntactic structures that impose high memory demands.

In recent years the body of research on aging has widened to include work on languages other than English, thus revealing effects of linguistic differences on cognitive processing. An example is the study by Gubarchuk and Kemper (1997) on the production of complex syntactic structures in Russian. They compared performance of young adult Russians visiting the US with that of older migrants in the US and young and older Russians in Moscow. Proficiency in Russian and scores on different syntactic structures appeared to be influenced much more by educational level and knowledge of English and other languages than by age. There was a clear effect of working memory, suggesting language specific effects of working memory limitations for complex structures that require storage of larger units for later processing.

Pragmatic aspects

With respect to discourse skills, there is some evidence to show that such skills increase with age: in particular, narrative skills have been judged to be superior for elderly speakers, but in discourse aiming at conveyance of information, elderly speakers have been found to be less effective. A negative aspect in intergenerational interactions is the tendency towards 'painful self-disclosures' (Coupland *et al.*, 1988). Such stories of pain and bereavement tend to maintain negative age stereotypes and may lead to reduced intergenerational contact and interaction which again may have negative effects on language use and well-being (see Chapter 3 for further discussion).

Summarizing the findings for language production in the healthy elderly, there are changes at the phonological level and in articulation and fluency that may lead to changes in social behavior. There is a tendency to avoid using complex sentences, but this is caused more by memory constraints than by a decline in syntactic skills as such. At the lexical level there are word-finding problems but these are found mainly for single word production and less so for words in context. For tasks like verbal fluency there is a clear effect of education: higher education seems to compensate for decline in access. Data on the Tip-of-the-Tongue phenomenon suggest that there also a speed of processing component in the differences between younger and older adults: when given enough time the latter group shows a pattern that is similar to that of the former group. On the pragmatic level older adults appear to show superior narrative skills but they are less effective in conveying information.

Language Comprehension

Phonological aspects

There is considerable research on the role of perception in the elderly and the role it plays in language comprehension. Kline and Scialfa (1996) present an overview of work on auditory and visual aging, and their main conclusions are that with aging there is a decline of sensitivity for tones with higher frequencies, a higher threshold for frequency recognition, and that this is increased in noisy environments, suggesting a decline in the ability to inhibit interference from the environment. Schneider *et al.* (2000) compared younger and older adults' performance in a discourse listening task in various levels of noise. For quiet and moderate noise conditions no difference was found between the two age groups, but only when the age-related hearing loss was compensated for. The authors conclude that speech comprehension difficulties of older adults primarily reflect declines in hearing rather than in cognitive ability (p. 110).

The findings on the role of peripheral perception are somewhat at odds with data from an ingenious experiment reported on by Lindenberger *et al.* (2001). They tested middle-aged adults under conditions of reduced visual acuity, auditory acuity or both. They reduced the acuity to the levels found in elderly people. These manipulations appeared to have no negative effect on cognitive performance compared to control conditions. They conclude that while perceptual problems may have an impact in the assessment of cognitive functioning there are still differences between the age groups that are not explained by these findings. Speed of processing may also be one of the factors explaining age-related problems in speech processing. Gordon-Salant and Fitzgibbons (2004) presented different age groups with normal and time compressed speech in different noise conditions. Elderly listeners showed lower scores under all noise conditions. The elderly listeners had more problems understanding the time compressed speech, which supports the generalized slowing hypothesis for aging.

Comprehension problems can be caused by processing problems at higher levels but they are also caused by decline in peripheral perception, such as hearing and vision. Schellstraete *et al.* (1998) looked at how young and elderly subjects read sentences in a self-paced reading task with immediate recall. The outcomes of their study show that the elderly group was both slower in reading and showing poorer recall. The results could be explained partly by working memory capacity. Reading can also be problematic by more peripheral problems. Gradual vision loss often coincides with aging. Reduced vision limits the possibilities for reading for pleasure and reading as part of normal activities of daily living. Ryan *et al.* (2003) carried out in-depth interviews with elderly people suffering from vision loss.

In comprehension of spoken sentences and discourse, intonation plays an important role. Sentence intonation can serve to disambiguate sentences like 'John said the main is late' which could have two interpretation: 'John said: 'The man is late' or 'John', said the man, 'is late'. Kjelgaard *et al.* (1999) looked at the use of prosodic cues in disambiguating sentences in groups of healthy young and elderly adults. Even though the intonational cues were often very subtle, both groups appeared to profit from them equally. This shows that the effective use of sentence prosody is well preserved in normal aging without extensive hearing problems. Prosody also plays a role in the expression of emotions. Thompson *et al.* (2001) show that a group of elderly people (mean age 77 years) had more problems differentiating intensity of emotions as expressed by prosody and facial expressions than a group of young adults (mean age 23).

Lexical aspects

The large volume of research on lexical aspects in language production is not matched by any similar set of studies on language comprehension. There are a number of studies on word recognition and word retrieval. Ratcliff *et al.* (2004) show that in a lexical decision task, older subjects are some 80–100 ms slower than younger subjects, but more accurate. There is a fairly large set of studies on priming effects, i.e. facilitating effects of either repeated presentation of the same word (repetition priming: bread – bread) or the presentation of a prime word that is phonologically or semantically related to the target word (head – bread / butter – bread). In a meta analysis of studies on phonological and semantic priming Laver and Burke (1993) showed that there are smaller semantic priming effects for younger than for older subjects. One explanation for this is that older subjects are slower and there is therefore more time for the priming effect itself and more room for speed-up due to the longer latencies; but one of the studies they reviewed used a deadline procedure that eliminated the effect of the longer latencies. The most likely solution is that through life-long experience elderly people have developed more semantic links between words and therefore the summation of the priming links between the words is larger than that of younger subjects. These assumptions are supported by the finding that there are age related declines in repetition priming (Burke *et al.*, 2000), so the differential effects for the two tasks must be attributed to differences in semantic structures. For other tasks, such as the drawing of inferences from reading and inferring meaning of unknown words from context, no age-related effects have been found. So for language comprehension at the lexical level there seems to be age constancy rather than change.

Syntactic aspects

Most studies have been concerned with the interaction between syntactical complexity and memory constraints. It is not always easy to compare studies and draw general conclusions, because the types of syntactic constructions used and their complexity vary considerably between studies. While the structures tested in the Lintsen and de Bot (1989) study reported above were fairly simple, and no effect of aging was found, other studies using more complex structures do show an age effect, though not all studies have taken into account the possible role of perception, memory and education as intervening variables. Kemtes and Kemper (1999) for instance, looked at the scope of quantifiers in comprehension ('Every actor used a prop' vs. 'An actor used every prop'). Different interpretations relate to different processing strategies. Immediate syntactic analysis appears not to be affected by aging or working memory whereas post-comprehension processes are affected by aging and/or working memory limitations.

Pragmatic aspects and reading comprehension

Most studies on language comprehension have used oral presentation of test material, probably because it is assumed that with confusion, vision and focus on written material becomes more problematic. Indeed, research shows that while reading aloud is relatively well preserved in demented patients, reading comprehension is poor. A few studies have looked at processing of text and discourse in elderly populations. Ulatowska *et al.* (1999) compared the processing of short fables in three groups, an older middle-age group (50–70 years), an old elderly group (> 80), and an aphasic group. Fables are interesting not only because it is a genre that is familiar and therefore not as artificial as many other experimental tests and texts, but also because there is a moral to convey. Finding the moral requires more than superficial processing of the text elements. The subjects had to retell the fables and give the gist of the story and the lesson or moral conveyed. The data show that the aphasics had lower scores on both measures, while there were no differences between the middle-aged and old elderly groups. The octogenarians also showed high levels of linguistic and communicative ability which was apparent in their use of metaphoric and proverbial language and complex syntactic structures. No information on level of education and present level of activity of the old elderly group was provided, but such data underline once more the variability in the older population and accordingly the risk of drawing general conclusions on the basis of selective samples.

Summarizing the findings on language comprehension, there seem to be clear effects of age on hearing and vision that have an impact on language perception. Perception of single tones and melodic lines declines with age. For lexical processing elderly subjects are slower in on-line tasks, but they seem to be more effective in using context information in processing words. Both working memory limitations and auditory sensory deficits appear to have an effect on the comprehension of complex syntax. Ambiguous sentences (like 'He hit the man with the sword') are more problematic than unambiguous ones, and more so for elderly people than education matched younger people. The same was found for noisy environments. Also rapid speech causes problems, and the various factors may interact to make comprehension more difficult, though it should be added that similar, though somewhat smaller effects, are found in younger populations. On the pragmatic level age-related effects have been found for reading comprehension, while oral presentation of text seems to reduce text comprehension considerably. Apart from these effects, language comprehension is generally well preserved in normal aging. Because older adults appear to be making optimal use of context the problems caused by hearing loss and reduced working memory capacity are generally compensated for adequately. This suggests that different subsystems interact to compensate for declining functioning of one of them. This could also be framed in terms of compensating resources since decline in memory is compensated by a stronger connectivity in the semantic system.

Language and Dementia

Before discussing the literature on language and dementia, it should be pointed out that 'dementia' as a label is used here rather loosely. There is a large literature on specific aspects and forms of dementia that show different symptoms. Also, there are levels of impairment ranging from very mild onset to complete silence and withdrawal. Decline is a gradual process and there do not seem to be clear stages that reflect specific bundles or configurations of symptoms. The research on language and dementia (and on language and aging generally) is basically static in nature, while we need a more dynamic perspective with a focus on development rather than steady states.

Language Production

Phonological aspects

There are only a few studies on phonological aspects of language production in dementia. Croot *et al.* (2000) analyzed conversational speech, single-word production and production of overpracticed series like the days of the week in patients with early dementia and found false start errors, phonological paraphasias and various signs of articulatory difficulties. Forbes *et al.* (2002) included articulation and melodic line in their analyses of picture descriptions by a group of Alzheimer patients and healthy controls. They found clear differences for aspects related to semantics, but few for articulation and phonology.

Lexical aspects

As with normal aging, there are various studies looking at lexical retrieval problems in AD patients. Nebes and Halligan (1998) compared younger and older participants and patients with probable Alzheimer's disease in experiments testing orthographic, phonological and semantic aspects of words. The patients showed longer latencies, but no differences in the types of decisions, which suggests that different aspects of lexical knowledge are well retained though more difficult to retrieve. Astell and Harley (1998) present data on picture naming and word picture matching. The data show that matching is easier than naming and that frequency and imageability play no role. As with normal elderly, the problem in word naming is the linking of the lexeme to the lemma rather than linking lexical concepts with the meaning part of the lexical item. This is in line with a study by Nicholas *et al.* (1996) on naming which claims that findings on semantic decline based on naming scores in AD patients are an artifact of scoring procedures.

Disruption of the ability to suppress competing but irrelevant information is likely to be one of the most prominent characteristics of the decline in dementia. Disinhibition is likely to be the cause of verbosity that is often associated with aging (Pushkar *et al.* 2000), but also with the word-finding problems and seemingly off-target language use found in cognitively impaired elderly people. The word-finding problems are probably not the result of access problems but of problems in the selection of the right (word) candidate.

Syntactic aspects

In a longitudinal study Kemper *et al.* (2001) looked at changes in linguistic ability in healthy older adults and adults with dementia. Healthy adults were tested using language samples, vocabulary tests and digit span tests every year, while the demented adults were tested twice a year. Grammatical complexity and propositional content appeared to decline in both healthy and demented adults, but the changes were faster in the demented group. They conclude that 'both grammatical complexity and propositional content are related to late-life changes in cognition in healthy older adults as well as those with dementia. Alzheimer's disease accelerates this decline, regardless of age' (p. 600). These findings point to a difference in decline between healthy and demented adults that is quantitative rather than qualitative in nature, suggesting the same underlying causes for the changes. In a study on sentence repetition with Alzheimer's patients, Small *et al.* (2000) found that AD patients had more problems repeating complex sentences with left and right branching of phrase structures and different verb-argument relations. There was a clear relation with working memory scores in this study.

In models of language production, monitoring plays a central role. A monitoring device is generally assumed to explain the fact that speech errors are often corrected. For language in dementia, one of the issues is, to what extent the language production system and the monitoring system are differentially affected. It might be the case that the production problems found in dementia are caused by the part of the system that generates speech, while the underlying implicit system of knowledge that is used in monitoring is still largely intact. Altmann *et al.* (2001) looked at speech errors in individuals with probable Alzheimer's disease and found that the same problems occurred in production and in detection and correction of speech errors. This suggests that the production and monitoring systems are equally affected.

Pragmatic aspects

With progression of the process of decline in dementia, the number and length of utterances decrease as well, therefore pragmatic aspects go down in number also. A number of longitudinal studies of pragmatic aspects in dementia (Hamilton 1994, Ripich *et al.*, 2000; Dijkstra *et al.*, 2004) have shown a lower frequency of cohesion and coherence building devices in patients with dementia and an increase in disruptive topic shifts and empty phrases. Despite this deterioration of pragmatic skills, dyads of patients with dementia and care givers show excellent skills in resolving communication breakdowns (Orange *et al.*, 1998).

Summarizing the findings on language production in pathological aging, there appears to be little research on phonology, which shows some decline on that level. For lexical aspects it turned out that patients with dementia are slower than age-matched controls but equally accurate. In word retrieval a decline in suppressing competing candidates is found regularly. For grammar a decline in grammatical complexity and propositional content is found. With dementia, monitoring appears to become less effective. On the pragmatic level it is found that there is a decline in the use of conversation building devices and more disruption of topics with the advancement of the dementia process. Conversational skills are retained relatively well, and verbal routines continue to be used till late stages of decline.

Perception

Phonological aspects

Research on phonological processing in patients with dementia seems to be limited to the relation between phonology and reading. Colombo *et al.* (2000) had patients read words with regular and irregular stress. Their data support earlier findings of a relatively unimpaired ability to translate orthography into phonology.

Lexical aspects

Semantic memory loss as evidenced by lexical decision with priming experiments have been reported in a number of studies (Bell *et al.* 2001; Balota *et al.*, 1999). Patients with dementia tend to show larger priming effects that can be explained partly by the other main finding that such patients are generally slower. As discussed earlier, the larger priming effects for elderly and demented subjects are a topic of debate at the moment. It is clear that patients with dementia continue to make use of context information for the comprehension of words. No research seems to have been done with lexical access when a larger context is provided.

Syntactic aspects

Most studies on language and dementia have been done with English, an exception is the study by Bickel *et al.* (2000) who looked at syntactic comprehension deficits in Alzheimer's patients in German. Using a sentence/picture matching test, they presented patients and matched controls with

sentences varying in complexity. The results show that the controls outperformed the patients on all sentence types, and that performance was not
related to age, but only to degree of cognitive decline. A comparison of
groups of patients with varying degrees of severity of impairment shows
that while syntactic comprehension is well maintained in the early stages of
dementia, it becomes more seriously affected in more advanced stages. As
in other studies, the explanation is sought in the reduction of working
memory capacity. In contrast to this, Croot *et al.* (1999) found that dementia
severity affected scores on sentence comprehension, but this could not be
explained by differences in working memory capacity. In their group of
very mild, mild and moderate dementia patients, the very mild group
showed impairments that were not found in the other groups, suggesting
that syntactic comprehension problems are more typical of onset of
dementia. A major problem is that the effects of complexity of the language
tested and the contribution of memory in the processing are difficult to
measure independently. In an ingenious study, Kempler *et al.* (1998) used
an on-line sentence comprehension task which aimed at minimizing the
memory requirements in performing the task. Their data show that in this
task, AD patients are able to process complex sentences and meanings.
They conclude that comprehension problems are limited when the
inability to maintain active information in memory is taken into account.

In an attempt to find out to what extent the underlying syntactic system
is affected in normal aging and Alzheimer's patients, Kemper (1997)
presented patients and matched controls with various sentence types and
asked them to make acceptability judgments. Both patients and controls
appeared to be affected by the extent to which the processing of the
sentences presented depended on working memory. For the patients, but
not the controls, metalinguistic judgments were affected by the loss of
semantic information about verbs.

Studies using neuro-imaging effects have added to our understanding
of underlying processes in language skills in the elderly. Grossman *et al.*
(2002) carried out a neuro-imaging study on sentence comprehension in
healthy and demented elderly adults and found significant differences
with respect to the regions of the brain involved in comprehension. Their
data suggest 'that these brain regions support an alternate, non-grammati-
cal strategy for processing complex configurations of symbolic
information' (p. 296).

While syntax may be relatively spared in dementia-type diseases, some
studies show that the overall decline of working memory also has its effect
on syntactic comprehension. Waters *et al.* (1998) presented patients with
dementia of the Alzheimer's type and matched normal controls with a
number of syntactic processing tasks in which comprehension was the

main issue. The findings show that complexity of the sentences used had little effect on the patients' performance, while the number of propositions in the sentences did have an effect. The explanation given is that this results from the need to store these propositions while processing other parts of the sentence, and a decline in working memory leads to a loss of this propositional meaning. Grossman and White-Devine (1998) looked at sentence comprehension and the role of syntax in a group of Alzheimer's patients, varying factors relating to syntax, semantics or other cognitive processing demands. In particular atypical syntactic-thematic mapping relations and selection restrictions associated with verbs appeared to cause difficulties. To what extent memory constraints played a role here, is not really clear.

Pragmatic aspects

While language decline has been claimed to be an early predictor of AD, few studies have actually tried to find what linguistic aspects differentiate between normal aging and early AD. Forbes *et al.* (2002) compared groups of minimal and mild AD patients with education-matched healthy controls with respect to a number of aspects of spontaneous speech using a simple and a complex picture description task. The analyses showed that only the complex task differentiated enough between the minimal AD patients and healthy controls. Semantic processing appeared to be the crucial differentiating factor. Most studies on language and dementia have been concerned with propositional language, and only very few with metaphoric use of language. Papagno (2001) looked at the comprehension of metaphors and idioms in patients with Alzheimer's disease and found no decline in the use of figurative language. This may point to a better retention of implicit knowledge as compared to explicit knowledge in AD.

It is not clear at what stage of dementia reading comprehension problems develop. Obler *et al.* (1999) report on a study in which they tested the effect of combining written and spoken input on comprehension in dementia. They compared comprehension using subtests of the Boston Diagnostic Aphasia Exam in three conditions: auditory input, written input and combined auditory/written input. The outcomes clearly show that comprehension is best in the combined condition, but that performance in the written condition is also significantly better than in the auditory condition. The effects were more pronounced with longer sentences as compared to shorter sentences, which suggests that the written input helped the patients to remember the sentences better and accordingly have more resources left to process them for comprehension. For diagnosis and therapy these findings are very relevant since the combination of modalities may make communication with the patients easier. This also points to specific problems for patients with no or low literacy.

While they cannot use the written input, they may be used to not having that and have therefore better heuristics to process auditory input. We will come back to this in the second part of this book.

Summarizing the findings on language perception in pathological aging, there appear to be too little data on phonological aspects to draw any conclusions. On the lexical level, word recognition is slower than in age-matched controls. Syntactic comprehension appears to be well-preserved in the early stage of dementia, in particular when memory constraints are cancelled out. Some problems in syntactic processing are actually caused by the loss of semantic and functional information. On the pragmatic level there appears to be little decline and text comprehension is well retained when the information is presented in both written and spoken form.

For language and dementia the effects found in normal aging seem to be aggravated. Therefore language may play a role in the early detection of dementia. According to Kemper *et al.* (1995) 'language impairments are secondary to motoric or mnemonic impairments but may constitute early markers of undiagnosed condition.' (p. 540).

Language-related Factors

Overlooking the main findings with respect to language skills, it becomes obvious that looking at language in isolation is not the right direction to take. Even though language as an overall skill can be decomposed into different subskills as presented in this chapter, the data also show that language processing is heavily dependent on other systems. From a DST perspective language development in aging and dementia should be studied by looking at how language and other systems co-evolve. Some other systems have been found to play a more important role in language use than others. The most important are the following:

- **Memory**
  While at first general memory performance was seen as the main factor, later on more specific working memory functions have been found to be associated with age, and to be more severely affected in dementia of the Alzheimer type. Various other functions ultimately result in changes of memory capacity (such as language proficiency and knowledge), making this the one dominant factor.
- **Auditory and visual perception**
  There is a steady decline of perception with age. This is not directly associated with dementia, though perception interacts with the ability to focus attention which is a problem even in the early stages of dementia.

- **Slowing down of cognitive functioning**
  While this type of decline can be compensated for, for instance by a reduced rate of input, it will have an effect on various cognitive tasks and everyday activities.
- **Education and advanced language skills**
  In practically all studies that have looked at the role of education this comes out as a very important factor: Higher levels of education are associated with less decline and fewer memory problems. Whether this is in fact a general effect of education or the result of more advanced linguistic skills is unclear. As we will point out in more detail in Chapter 5, linguistic skills and memory performance are strongly related.
- **Inhibition capacity**
  A reduction of the inhibition capacity may lead to both verbosity in production and a slowing down of language production and decline in language comprehension because of the inability to suppress irrelevant candidates in selection processes.

In this chapter we have tried to summarize the vast literature on language use and language skills in both healthy and demented elderly. For language production, change with age has been found at the phonological and lexical level. There may be changes at the syntactical level, but these probably interact with changes in memory capacity. There is also a decline in speed of processing that may suggest a decline in the language system, but given enough time the slowing down of the system can be overcome. For language comprehension, changes in memory capacity and decline in auditory and visual perception appear to be more prevalent than purely linguistic changes. Generally, language comprehension is well preserved in normal aging.

In the next chapter we will look at these other systems that act as resources for language production and perception in more detail.

Chapter 5

Resources in Language and Aging

In this chapter some of the resources that play a role in language development in the elderly population will be discussed. In a dynamic system, resources are needed to keep the system going: without resources the system will lose its flow of energy and come to a standstill. However, the connectivity and interactivity that are essential characteristics of dynamic systems imply that what counts as a resource is only relative to a specific developing aspect. To be more concrete: orthographic skills can be considered to be a resource for reading comprehension, so when we are interested in the development of reading comprehension, we can look at the role of orthographic skills as one of the resources. But only a slight change of perspective can reverse the roles: when we are interested in the development of orthographic skills, reading comprehension can be seen as a resource for that process, because better reading comprehension skills will enhance letter and word reading as well. Van Geert (1994) distinguishes between an intrinsic learning function that describes the gain in mastery or skills for a specific variable, and external resources, but he stresses that these resources are only relative to the variable at issue. Therefore it is better to talk about the learning function and the resources than about dependent and independent variables. The learning function we are primarily interested in here is language development.

Throughout this book we have looked at language as a system. If we are interested in the relation between the development of language as a system or rather as a variable, we define the system at the highest level of aggregation. Language is part of the larger cognitive system, which in itself is part of an individual mental system. This again resides in the body of an individual who is part of a larger community and so on. So the individual is both a dynamic system by itself with bodily and mental subsystems interacting, and as such he or she is part of various larger dynamic systems on the social plane: family, friends, Nordic Folkboat owners, research communities and so on. Here we want to limit the discussion to language as a system which can be subdivided in subsystems at different levels that in themselves again can be subdivided. To give an example: the articulatory system is one of the subsystems of the language production system, but within the articulatory system there are articulatory units or motor programs that are in themselves again dynamic systems (Browman & Goldstein, 1995). The state of a given subsystem is defined by the combined state of all the subsystems that constitute that larger system, and changes in that overall state reflect changes in one or more of the subsystems. Since all subsystems as interrelated, change in one means change in all. To go back to the articulation example: changes in the motor program for the production of one particular sound unit means that all other motor programs change as well, if only because for smooth articulation the linking of motor programs to sound units must fit.

The relative status of resources makes a discussion of general effects of resources in development somewhat problematic. Still, we think it can be argued that a number of external resources will play a role in the development of the language system as a whole and in most if not all of its subsystems. We will try to show this by exploring the role of memory in language production later on. In order to limit the number of potential resources we will only look at those that have been reported in the language and aging literature. This has led to the following list:

- Working memory capacity and long term memory capacity.
- Attentional processes.
- Speed of processing.
- Education.
- The social and linguistic environment.
- Multilingualism.

The degree of reciprocity of the relation between language development and the resources varies: while it is obvious that changes in language proficiency will have an impact on the linguistic environment, multilingualism and to a lesser extent working memory capacity, proficiency will not have an effect on education over the life span because we cannot change the past. Still the relation may not be completely uni-directional: e.g. relearning a language is more effective than learning a language from scratch (de Bot & Stoessel, 2000), so a learning action now has an impact on what is considered the outcome of the past educational process.

Before we discuss the various types of resources, we first need to get into more detail about what constitutes language in our perspective and how different types of resources can be related to specific aspects of the language system.

Decline of Language Skills and Other Behavioral Changes

In this specific context, it is not really clear what 'language' is. In the previous chapters the terms language and language skills have been used rather loosely. In order to link the resources to language skills we need a model of language that is sufficiently detailed to make that link. We are primarily interested in what the language system consists of and what it can do. Here, language use is seen as a very advanced and complex skilled behavior. Skills develop with use, and decline with non-use. The basic skills may be quite resistant to decline, like our abilities to ride a bicycle or swim. Once we have learned them we don't forget the basics. But for doing more advanced things quickly and properly, exercise is needed. In a way using language is like top sports: it is complex, extremely fast and calls for integration of many different skills. The complex parts of those skills need to be trained regularly to maintain them, otherwise they atrophy and fade, and are difficult to reactivate. In the last decades psycholinguistic research has accumulated that informs us about the different components of language skills.

So far, research on language, aging and dementia tends to be fragmentary in the sense that isolated aspects of language are tested without reference to a comprehensive model of language processing. In the next section one such model is presented and discussed with reference to resource capacity.

Levelt's 'Speaking' Model

The dominant language production model at the moment is Levelt's 'Speaking' model. Here a very short description of the model with a particular emphasis of aspects of memory will be given. (for extensive descriptions see Levelt, 1989, 1993, Levelt *et al.*, 1999). The backbone of the human language production (and perception) system is formed by the relations between three distinct levels of representation: the conceptual level, the lemma level and the word form level. In production the communicative intentions are formatted by the conceptualizer (to use Levelt's terms) in such a way that they can be handled by the formulator. At the conceptual level two stages are distinguished: macroplanning and microplanning. Macroplanning 'involves the elaboration of some communicative goal into a series of sub-goals, and the retrieval of the information to be expressed in order to realize each of those sub-goals' while microplanning 'assigns the right propositional shape to each of these 'chunks' of information' (1989: 11). The outputs of the conceptualizer are so-called 'preverbal messages'; in other words messages which contain all the necessary information to convert meaning into language, but which are not themselves linguistic. In the formulator the preverbal message is converted into a speech plan (phonetic plan) by selecting the right words/lexical units and applying grammatical and phonological rules.

In the model production takes place 'from left to right', i.e. the next processor will start working on the output of the current processor even if this output is still incomplete. In addition, there is no need to continually look back in time to see what has already been produced. This means that when a part of an utterance has left the conceptualizer and is being formulated, it cannot in any way influence the construction of parts that follow: each part of the utterance that leaves the conceptualizer passes through the whole system more or less by itself, without taking account of what may follow later on. Furthermore, production is incremental, so as soon as the information which goes with one part of the utterance is passed on to the formulator, the conceptualizer doesn't wait for that chunk to go through the whole system but immediately starts on the next part. In this way various parts of the same sentence will be at different processing stages: when the first part is being produced by the articulator, the last part may not have left the conceptualizer. Consequently the different components are at work simultaneously. Processing is largely automatic. Greatest attention is paid to conceptualizing and some attention is paid to the feedback mechanisms, but the remainder functions without conscious control. Production has to be incremental, parallel and automatized in order to account for the enormous speed at which language is produced. The incremental and parallel nature of language production means that the different sub-processes have to be synchronized in such a way that the output of a module becomes available at the right moment to be processed by the next module. This calls for buffering in all stages of processing.

Memory in Language Processing

For the generation of a sentence a number of steps can be distinguished. The links between the modules in the model are typically the sites at which elements have to be selected and processed for the next module:

(1) For language production information from long-term memory is needed: information about the topic, what is given and new, and what is the communicative setting. This is included in the Discourse Record which is part of Working Memory.
(2) The communicative intention and the communicative message have to be stored in order to allow for monitoring of the output.
(3) The activation of the lemma leads to both selection of the lexeme from the lexicon and to the activation of specific syntactic procedures that are triggered by syntactic role information in the lemma. For the gener-

ation of a surface structure different elements with their specific syntactic roles have to 'find each other' and the ones coming in first have to be stored until all the elements needed to set up the syntactic frame aimed at are available.

(4) In order to arrive at the phonological spell-out, the slots in the syntactic frames have to be filled with the lexemes selected. Again the lexemes need to be stored because the construction of the surface structure may not have the same timing as the lexeme selection process, and the lexemes may not be called upon in the same order as they have been selected in an earlier stage.

(5) Metrical spell-out information and segmental spell-out information have to be synchronized as input for the prosody generator, which calls for buffers for these to subcomponents.

(6) Address frames and segmental spell-out for phonological words have to be synchronized for the formation of phonological words. Therefore storage of elements from the two components may be needed for some time.

The description given here is already a very reduced summary of the complete blueprint of the speaker, but it is obvious that for fluent speech the subcomponents have to provide their output at the right time and any disruption in one of the many subprocesses will lead to a breakdown of the flow of speech.

One particularly important aspect of memory is the span of attention or the ability to work on a number of different notions at the same time. The attention span is typically limited, but it can become larger when the infor-mation is structured. This is not limited to language use: an expert chess player may be able to attend all chess-pieces in a game at the same time, while a beginning chess player can only attend two or three. For language, span of attention and skill in the language are related: a learner of a foreign language may be able to attend to a small stretch of speech only while a native speaker can handle much longer stretches. This means that decline of language skills has an effect on span of attention. In language production attention is focused more on macro planning and micro planning: the gen-eration of intention and messages, and less on lower level procedures. Working memory capacity has to be divided between monitoring the speaker's own internal and external speech, and different aspects of the discourse setting. Since this is not a module specific memory task, something like Baddeley's Central Executive may emerge as a solution.

In the Levelt model, the monitor plays an important role as a control system. Self-monitoring of external and internal speech involves both parsed and verbatim storage of all utterances for the time needed to check the form chosen with the original message. External speech has also to be included in the Discourse Record. Note that the Discourse Record is not a tape-recoding of actual speech as it happened. It is the speaker's internal representation of the discourse in which the language used and other types of information interact. Levelt (1989: 21) claims that working memory is the resource for monitoring.

Some general points with respect to memory emerge from the discussion given above: in different stages of language processing, memory capacity and language skills interact, this holds for information in the phonological loop, but also for span of attention in production and perception. A straight causal relation going from memory decline to language problems is therefore too simple, but it is obvious that without sufficient buffering capacity the language production system will stop functioning.

While the Levelt model is one of the dominant models at the moment, and it has been very effective in explaining many aspects of language production on monolinguals and bilinguals (de Bot, 2004; de Bot & Schreuder, 1993), some of the basic aspects of the model do not go well with a DST approach to language and language development. It is beyond the scope of the present chapter to go into any detail here, but the assumptions about representations and algorithms to process them are at odds with some of the basic principles of dynamic systems according to some researchers in the field (Crutchfield, 1998; van Gelder, 1998).

Working Memory Capacity and Long Term Memory Capacity

In the previous section we focused on specific aspects of memory in language production. Here we want to discuss more general aspects of memory. Traditionally a distinction is made between long-term memory and short-term memory. Long-term memory contains all sorts of permanent knowledge. Morris and Gruneberg (1994: 35) list various divisions of long-term memory that have been proposed. One of the most influential divisions is the one by Tulving (1972) between episodic memory (memory for events) and semantic memory (memory for facts). A further development was the division of semantic memory into procedural memory ('knowing how') and declarative of propositional memory ('knowing that'). Short-term memory was viewed as a static temporary store till Baddeley (1986) developed his Working Memory model. According to this model, the different parts of Working Memory not only store information, but also process and manipulate them. This model (see Baddeley, 1986 and Gathercole & Baddeley, 1993 for detailed accounts) is arguably the best developed and empirically supported model of Working

Memory available. It consists of a general purpose processing unit, the Central Executive, with two slave systems: the Phonological Loop and the Visuo-spatial Sketch Pad. While the various functions of the 'slave systems' in language processing are rather clear, in particular the phonological loop as a system that serves as a temporary store of linguistic information, the Central Executive's role is less clearly defined. Linking the Baddeley model of Working Memory to current models of language processing in production and perception is problematic because of a very fundamental difference in perspective on the working of the brain. While most processing models take a modular perspective with dedicated modules that carry out specialized tasks, Baddeley's Central Executive is a general purpose system. In their discussion of the role of working memory in language production, Gathercole and Baddeley point out this problem: 'The notion that a general purpose production system, such as the central executive, contributes to speech production does not sit comfortably with this modular perspective' (1993: 93). For their discussion of language production, Gathercole and Baddeley make use of Garrett's (1980) model, which is at the basis of more recent models such as the now dominant Levelt (1989, 1993) model that has been discussed in the previous section. Gathercole and Baddeley suggest that the Central Executive may play a role in temporal storage at higher levels of processing in language production (in Garrett's terms the message and functional level) rather than at the lower sound and articulation levels. How temporary storage at those levels takes place remains unclear because Gathercole and Baddeley present evidence that the phonological loop is *not* involved in that type of temporary storage. Levelt's position on this is clear; 'Intermediate representations, such as preverbal messages, surface structures, and the phonetic plan, have their own kinds of units; there is no *single* unit of processing in the production of speech (1989: 28, his italics). For the purposes of this contribution this 'mismatch' is problematic in the sense that most of the research in working memory and language deficits uses a variant of Baddeley account of Working Memory as a basis. Task-specific memory systems of buffers cannot be easily integrated in such a view.

In contrast to the Central Executive, the idea of a phonological loop can be accommodated in the type of models of language processing we will be discussing here. In language perception, the phonological loop plays an important role in storing bits of speech that cannot be processed on-line. Comprehension problems arise when the processing of incoming speech becomes so slow that the input that is temporarily stored in the phonological loop overloads the storing capacity. This means that parts of the input are lost unanalyzed (Kempler *et al.*, 1998). Fisk and Warr (1996) looked at the contribution of perceptual speed, the Central Executive and the phonological loops in explaining age-related differences in information processing. No age effect was found for the phonological loop, which undermines the explanation given above, while perceptual processing was the variable explaining most of the variance. There are two possibilities for explaining the relation between language and memory: one is that the capacity of both the processing units of the speech comprehension system and the storage capacity of the phonological loop decline, with an impact on language processing. The other possibility is that a decline in language skills has an impact on processing and storage capacity. Following suggestions made by Snowdon *et al.* (1996) it could be hypothesized more generally that linguistic ability acts as a buffer to cognitive decline by facilitating mnemonic processes for encoding, organizing and retrieving information. O'Hanlon *et al.* (2001) point to the distinction between implicit and explicit memory in research on aging. Implicit memory is generally found to be more resistant to the effects of aging than explicit memory, which is reflected in problems in the elderly in consciously learning new information. It is quite likely that many of the effects of aging on memory can be explained by looking at the type of memory and learning involved. The implicit/explicit distinction also plays a role in lexical processing and lexical acquisition in AD patients. Grossman *et al.* (1997) showed in a learning experiment with AD patients that they could learn a new word's grammatical form class, but had difficulty acquiring the new word's lexical meaning. This distinction can be interpreted as a difference between explicit (semantic meaning) and implicit (grammatical word form) learning.

Norman *et al.* (1991) tested elderly people's comprehension and recall of complex sentences. As predicted there was a decline in the processing of the more complex sentences in particular for elderly people with reduced working memory capacity. What is interesting, though, is that in the correlational analysis, the effect of age on processing was not significant when working memory capacity (digit span) was controlled for. While there was a significant correlation between age and backward digit span (in which informants have to recall a series of digits in reversed order of presentation) no significant correlation with forward digit span was found. This suggests that the relation between age and processing decline is very weak and is mediated by specific limitations in working memory.

The role of working memory in reading was studied by Brebion (2003) who found that when elderly readers run out of resources, they sacrifice mnemonic resources to devote more resources to processing. Age-related differences between episodic and semantic memory were reported by Nyberg *et al.* (2003). Recall appears to be more affected than recognition and episodic memory is more age sensitive than semantic memory. The role of working memory and processing speed in skilled performance by different age groups was studied by Brigman and Cherry (2002). They conclude that both factors play a role, but they stress the fact that there are considerable individual differences, in particular with respect to processing speed. In addition to behavioral measures, there are now also studies using neuro-imaging techniques to relate memory performance and changes in the brain. In an MRI-based study on volume of brain structures, in particular the medial temporal lobe, Petersen *et al.* (2000) showed that differences in volume can predict reliable differences in memory and language performance in probable Alzheimer's patients and normal control subjects. These findings provide a neuro-anatomical basis for the assumption of decline in memory performance.

One of the few studies that include three of the factors discussed here (working memory capacity, speed of processing and inhibition) in one design is a study by Van der Linden *et al.* (1999). They studied the effects of these three factors in isolation and combined in a group of 151 subjects aged 31–80. The subjects completed tests for language processing and different tasks measuring speed of processing, memory performance and resistance to interference. The latent construct equation model with the best fit was the one in which the contributions of speed of processing and resistance to interference are indirect and mediated by working memory, which appears to be the key component in explaining age-related changes in language performance (see also Radvansky, 1999 and See & Ryan, 1995 for similar findings).

Attentional Processes and Inhibitory Control

As various authors have indicated (Juncos-Rabadán & Iglesias, 1994; Croot *et al.*, 2000; Small *et al.*, 2000), the ability to focus attention is part of the resources in language use. Attention may compensate for a decline in perception and memory capacity. Closely related to attention is the notion of age-related disinhibition, i.e. an increased inability to inhibit irrelevant information. In this view the slowing down is partly a result of competition in selection processes: too many – partly irrelevant – candidates present themselves, which slows down the selection process. The inhibition deficit hypothesis has been mentioned as one of the age-related mechanisms that have a negative effect on different aspects of language production and perception because it causes interference and noise in various parts of the language system. Cameli and Phillips (2000) tested this hypothesis in a neuro-imaging study using the N400 ERP in a priming paradigm. Sentence contexts and word primes were either highly related, moderately related or unrelated to the target. Results show that young adults (aged 19–29) were more sensitive to the priming effect, showing the expected N400 effect for unrelated pairs, whereas the older group (aged 62–88) showed no sensitivity to priming and accordingly no N400 effect. These findings support the inhibition deficit in older adults. Burke *et al.* (2000) have challenged the explanatory power of the inhibition deficit hypothesis on the grounds that its effects should be equally visible in language production and perception, while age effects in perception are far smaller than in production. Burke *et al.* suggest that rather than general all-purpose mechanisms that can explain only part of the findings on language in aging they should be replaced by more specific, maybe even task specific, mechanisms.

Role of Education

Education is a resource that is clearly different from other types of resources. It reflects both a set of knowledge acquired through formal education and a set of skills in acquiring knowledge in a specific structured way. Just as 'language', 'education' is a dynamic set of variables of various kinds. And like inhibition, it is likely to play a role in different ways for different tasks. For example, for tests like phonological fluency in which subjects have to list as many words as possible beginning with a specific letter, having a large vocabulary, which is one of the typical results of going through higher level of education, plays a role. Education becomes relevant when a given skill has been acquired or used frequently in educational processes.

The general finding for word and picture naming is that it declines with age, starting in the 30s and speeding up in the 70s to 80s range, but there appears to be enormous individual variation with some individuals in their 70s performing similar to much younger controls. Level of education has been found to be a major factor in explaining individual differences in naming (Bayles & Kaszniak, 1987; Au *et al.*, 1990). Barresi *et al.* (1999) tried to explain these individual differences by looking at language related activities of elderly people in a longitudinal study covering 10 years. Ages ranged from 40s to mid-80s. The subjects selected had no history of neurological or psychiatric disorder, and their number of years of education ranged from 7 to 25. The subjects were asked to fill out a questionnaire on frequency of language related activities like reading and writing for pleasure or profession, computer use, foreign languages, and television viewing. Performance on the Boston Naming Test was used as the dependent variable. There was a significant negative correlation between naming performance and age, and a significant positive relation between naming performance and level of education. In a multiple regression analyses the only language use related variable that made a unique contribution to the explanation of variance was the amount of TV watching: more time spent on TV watching was associated with lower naming scores. Similar results with respect to the role of education in normal aging are reported by Ardila *et al.* (2000) who found that in groups of participants with different ages and levels of education, 'test scores were strongly associated with level of education, and differences among age groups were smaller than differences among education groups' (p. 495). Another interesting outcome from their study was that for more poorly educated participants, optimal performance on neuropsychological tests was reached at an older age than for more highly educated groups. Why less education leads to differential effects in aging is not really clear. Bosma *et al.* (2003) present an interesting perspective in their study on the impact of working conditions on cognitive decline in later life. In a longitudinal study they found that work-related challenges and mental stimuli explain some 42% of the variance in the education effects in aging. So the effect of education in their view is not a direct one, but comes out as a result of the less varied and challenging work conditions of people with lower levels of education.

Speed of Processing

Speed of processing has been mentioned regularly as one of the variables that explain differences between age groups and individuals in age groups. There is sufficient evidence to support the view that there is a general slowing down of processing with aging, but it is less clear when and how that slowing down actually leads to problems in language use. Wingfield *et al.* (2001) set up an experiment to test the hypothesis that given enough time to process, the elderly will show results similar to other age groups. For this they allowed younger and older adults to control the speed of delivery of spoken prose that was to be recalled later. No differences between groups were found. This shows that the processing mechanisms are working properly, and that the decline in speed of processing can be compensated for by a slowing down of the input. Pichora-Fuller (2003) found age-related differences in auditory temporal processing and speed of cognitive processing. She concludes that some of the problems in age-related hearing and comprehension problems are related with auditory temporal processing rather than higher cognitive abilities.

Processing speed may also be related to fluid intelligence. Zimprich and Martin (2002) found age-related decline in both processing speed and fluid intelligence and a correlation of 0.53 between the two in a cross-sectional study of different age groups. In a longitudinal study by the same authors (Martin & Zimprich, 2002) a much weaker relation between the mental speed and intelligence was found. Salthouse (2000) has argued that differences in 'pure' measures of speed of processing show a high correlation with tasks in which a component of speed is present, suggesting that many cognitive processes are affected by changes in speed. How speed of processing, inhibition efficiency and working memory capacity interact is not clear. Van der Linden *et al.* (1999) found that in their analyses working memory was the most important factor in explaining differences between age groups, while See and Ryan (1995) found that inhibitory efficiency and processing speed were stronger as factors.

The Social and Linguistic Environment

In the DST approach, the link between the social plane and the psychological plane is crucial. All resources together, both the intra-individual ones and the inter-individual ones form what van Geert (1994) calls the 'cognitive ecosystem' of an individual. The term 'ecosystem' nicely reflects that fact that the individual is part of a larger system with which she interacts. For our discussion language and aging we will focus on a changes in the social and linguistics setting with aging.

As discussed in Chapter 3, several cues play a role in the perception and categorization of individuals according to age. Again, it is beyond the scope of this chapter to discuss the vast sociological literature on stereotyping and aging. As far as language is concerned, linguistic behavior plays an important role in defining people as old, both by young people and by elderly people themselves. Ryan *et al.* (1992) found that both young and old adults expected the old to have more language-related problems, apart from two skills: telling enjoyable stories and being sincere when talking. In a follow-up study, Hummert *et al.* (1995) found the same stereotyping effect, but not the positive effects for the two skills mentioned in the Ryan *et al.* (1992) study. Vocal characteristics appear to be reliable indicators of age, and other aspects, such as pauses and hesitations, are interpreted as signs of cognitive slowing down. While age is generally seen as an acceptable excuse for memory failures in older adults, and can relieve awkward social situations, the strategy to use age as an excuse still contributes to a negative age stereotyping (Ryan *et al.*, 2002). At the same time, memory failures are seen as typical of old age (Bieman-Copland & Ryan, 1998).

Apart from stereotypes of elderly in terms of cognitive functioning, elderly people are often seen as being frail and dependent on care. As indicated earlier, the recent emergence of the concept of the 'golden ager' has on the one hand corrected that picture in a positive sense, but at the same time it has made the non-golden ager even more pitiful.

Analyses of interactions with elderly people have revealed a couple of things (see Chapter 3 for more details). One is that intergenerational communication can be problematic, though this is felt more so by the elderly people themselves than by their younger counterparts. The other is that elderly people are often spoken to in a very specific way. From research on the effects of elderspeak, it is clear that depending on how alert they are perceived, elderly people are often confronted with a specific register of talk that is not unlike baby-talk or foreigner talk. All of these registers are characterized by a slower speaking rate, more exaggerated intonation, the use of simple words and constructions and the enhanced use of diminutives and personal pronouns. There appear to be two motives for the use of such a register: to overcome communication problems, that is, to improve the transmission of information; and to express care and concern, and to enhance personal relations, So, the right type of elderspeak, affective but not too patronizing, avoiding semantic and syntactic complexity, is both effective in improving comprehension and is valued positively by elderly people. The wrong type of elderspeak, condescending, and more care taker-talk like with a low speech rate and exaggerated intonation and over-short and choppy sentences – is detrimental to communication, is devalued and leads to a decline in self-respect in elderly people.

As the studies mentioned here and in Chapter 3 show, there are age-related changes in attitudes towards individuals. Age-related physical and cognitive changes are assumed and younger people adapt their behavior in various ways. This means that the cognitive ecosystem of the elderly individual changes along with the other changes taking place in this phase of life. All these processes of change interact and they need to be considered in combination rather than in isolation.

Language as a Resource in Cognitive Aging: The 'Nun'-study

Though the focus in this chapter is on the impact of other resources on language, there are also strong indications that language skills can act as a resource for other cognitive skills. One of the highlights in research on cognitive functioning and aging is the so-called 'Nun'-study (Snowdon, 1997, Snowdon *et al.* 1996). In this unique study 93 nuns of the School Sisters of Notre Dame congregation agreed to have yearly neuropsychological evaluations and to donate their brains at death. The congregation is active in various types of education, and all of its members are trained as teachers. All participants made their handwritten autobiographies which they had written around the beginning of their training available: 47 of the 93 sisters wrote new autobiographies in 1995, so providing unique material for a longitudinal evaluation of their linguistic skills between 1930 and 1995. In the analyses of the autobiographies two indicators were concentrated on: Idea

Density (ID, defined as the average number of ideas per 10 words), and Grammatical Complexity (GC, based on a Developmental Level metric which classifies sentences at one of eight levels of complexity). Cognitive functioning was assessed with a battery of seven standard tests, including fluency tests, recall and recognition, Boston Naming and the Mini-mental State Exam. The neuropathological evaluation looked at senile plaques and neurofibrillary tangles in different brain regions.

The results show a significant correlation between scores for ID and GC, and a significant correlation between years of education and ID. No relation was found with age at which the autobiography was written, or the age of the assessment or cognitive functioning, while there was a significant relation between cognitive functioning, ID, GC, and years of education. One of the most important findings was that there was a strong association between ID and GC in early life and scores on cognitive functioning in later life. Of the 93 nuns in the larger sample, 14 died and, and their brains have been examined along with those of nuns from another convent, 25 nuns, of whom 10 had confirmed Alzheimer's disease (AD). It turned out that low ID was found in 90% of the nuns with AD and only 13% for those without AD. Also the nuns with low ID had more neurofibrillary tangles in the hippocampus than those with high ID. Snowdon *et al.* (1996) hypothesize that there may be a relation between low linguistic ability in early life and the expression of dementia. The authors suggest that high linguistic ability in early life may function as a 'neurological reserve capacity' which acts as a buffer to cognitive decline because the linguistic skills allow more efficient strategies for storing and retrieving information (see Chapter 4 for a discussion of working memory capacity and linguistic skills). Then there are two possibilities: either low linguistic abilities are very early signs of the onset of AD, or low linguistic abilities accelerate the development of AD.

The idea of linguistic capacity as a buffer or compensation for neurological changes is also central in the description by Snowdon (1997) of one of the heros of the nun-studies, Sister Mary. She became a trained teacher in the course of her career and was teaching full time till she was 77 and part-time till she was 84. After her retirement she remained active in the community. She died at the age of 101.7 years. She had had her last functional assessment just eight months prior to her death and was assessed as being cognitively intact (27 out of 30 on the MMSE). Post-mortem analysis of her brain showed abundant neurofibrillary tangles and senile plaques, which are normally associated with dementia. In that sense she was a good example of the possible compensatory mechanism of linguistic ability for brain damage.

Multilingualism

As mentioned earlier, it is not clear yet to what extend multilingualism is an asset or a liability in aging and accordingly to what extent is can be seen as a resource. Having more languages can act as a repository of linguistic skills and knowledge that can be drawn from when using language. We have already discussed the potential role of multiple languages in testing and treatment for decline. Knowing more languages will only be an asset when these languages are relevant in the setting the elderly individual is in, but it has also been argued (Herdina & Jessner, 2002) that knowledge of multiple languages leads to more advanced metalinguistic skills that may be relied on in using any language. So there may be a positive effect of multilingualism in language proficiency. But multilingualism may also have an effect on other types of cognitive processing. In a ground-breaking article, Bialystok *et al.* (2004) report on a study in which they looked at possible advantages of life-long bilingualism in aging. Building on earlier work showing that bilingual children perform better on various cognitively demanding tasks, they tested the hypothesis that such advantages could continue to play a role in adulthood and even help to counter cognitive decline. Their argument is basically this: bilinguals who use more than one language on a daily basis have to keep their languages apart all the time. It is generally accepted now that bilinguals cannot simply switch off languages in processing: while speaking one language, the other languages are processed as well, so there is competition between languages within the language production system (Hermans *et al.* 1998; Francis, 1999). So the inhibitory control mechanisms of bilinguals have to be well developed which also has an effect on other cognitive tasks. In the experiments reported by Bialystok *et al.* (2004) younger (mean age = 40) and an older (mean age = 71) monolingual and bilingual (English/Tamil) groups had to perform a non-linguistic task requiring speeded reactions to congruent and incongruent information. The data show a clear effect of bilingualism in both age groups: they responded more rapidly to conditions that placed greater demands on working memory. In the older group the advantage of bilingualism was even greater than in the younger group. These findings suggest that the life-long training of keeping languages apart has a positive effect on cognitive functioning not just for languages but more generally.

Conclusions

In this chapter we discussed several types of resources that may play a role in language development in aging. The most obvious are memory, inhibition, speed of processing and education; but in addition to these intra-individual resources, there are also extra-individual or social resources, such as the social and linguistic environment and multilingualism at the individual and the group level. In line with DST principles, we assume that all these resources interact with language as a skill. In the final chapter we will have closer look at this interacting and propose a model that takes into account the role of various resources and their role in and interaction with language proficiency.

Chapter 6

Multilingualism, Aging and Dementia

Bilingualism and multilingualism are the rule and monolingualism is the exception in most parts of the world. In that sense the literature discussed in the previous chapters is heavily biased. Research on language and aging is dominated by researchers in North America, and it is very rare to find even the slightest suggestion of a role for more than one language in that research. Whether the age groups studied are in fact really monolingual we don't know. Information on knowledge of other languages is not commonly provided. So it may be true that all of those individuals were monolinguals and it is just the researchers' monolingual bias that shows. Worldwide, a monolingual perspective is not just a bias, it is simply the wrong perspective. In this chapter we want to show why and how we should study more than one language in our research on aging. We will try to show how a multilingual perspective follows naturally from adopting a dynamic systems view on language development. In the following chapters we will discuss a number of projects on language and aging in multilinguals settings, and in that sense the present chapter serves as a bridge between the theoretical Chapters 2 to 6 and the more data-based Chapters 7 to 9.

For the study of language and aging in multilingual settings we need to make a broad distinction between multilingualism at the societal level and at the individual level. Multilingual societies do not necessarily consist of individuals who are themselves multilinguals. Quite often it is a situation of groups that speak their own language but also the language of the country or region they live in. These groups are typically minority groups whose culture and language have a lower status than the dominant language. At the individual level, there are different types of multilingualism. Individuals can vary with respect to age of acquisition of their different languages, the setting in which they acquired the language (as second or a foreign language), the levels of proficiency in different skills, degree of retention of languages not used, attitudes towards various languages and so on.

In this chapter we will present basically all the research we could find on healthy aging and multilingualism, which is not that much. Then we will discuss the literature on dementia and multilingualism, and relate the findings on multilingualism to a dynamic systems perspective. In the second part of this chapter we will discuss some of the specific problem in testing language and aging in multilingual and multicultural societies and groups.

A Dynamic Systems Perspective on Second Language Acquisition and Multilingualism

A number of publications have argued for a dynamic systems approach to second language acquisition (SLA) and multilingualism. Larsen-Freeman (1997) and Herdina and Jessner (2002) are the two publications that have laid the foundation of this line of research. More recently, the Groningen Applied Linguistics group has related dynamic systems to SLA and multilingualism in a number of publications (de Bot *et al.*, 2005, Lowie *et al.*, 2005, Verspoor *et al.*, 2004). They point to several aspects of multilingual systems as dynamic systems and show that many of the characteristics of dynamic systems as discussed in Chapter 2 also apply to such systems. One of the crucial issues is that different languages are in fact subsystems of the larger language system and that these subsystems are interrelated on different levels. The other issue is that as languages develop, their development has an impact on other languages. So if someone learns a second or third language, this will inevitably have an effect on the other languages in the system, including the first language. As discussed earlier, dynamic systems depend on resources that are by definition limited and that have to be shared by different subsystems. Therefore growth in one language may imply decline in another language. Also, assuming that the total amount of resources for the language system is more or less bounded, the resources for each language in the multilingual will be less than those for the single language in a monolingual.

The languages in a multilingual may be more or less related: English and German show more structural overlap than English and Mandarin, and so the systems will differ in connectedness. It may be easier to maintain a set of related languages like Dutch, German and Danish than a more disparate set like English, Xhosa and Afrikaans. At the same time, the risks of interference between related language is much larger than that between unrelated languages.

One of the central tenets in the application of DST to cognition is that the individual's cognition is shared, situated and embodied, which means that cognition, and accordingly language, is not a commodity residing somewhere in the brain isolated from other parts of the body or the environment, but that it is linked to the physical and social environment the individual is in. As we showed in chapter 3, the social environment in aging may be crucial for understanding part of the changes in cognition and the other way around.

Aging and second/foreign language skills

A basic question is whether multilingualism is an asset or a liability in aging. There is at least one theory that predicts more decline with aging in a second or third language than in the first language. Paradis's *A Neurolinguistic Theory of Bilingualism* (Paradis, 2004) claims that the L1 is learned implicitly for the larger part, while most people acquire their second language in an explicit way. This is particularly true for foreign language learners who learn the other languages through instruction. As mentioned before, aging appears to have more of an effect on explicit memory than on implicit memory. Since the second languages depend more on explicit knowledge, they will be more vulnerable than the first language. In other words it is not a specific effect of first vs. later learned languages *per se*, but the way in which such languages have been acquired. It would be worth exploring to what extent second languages that have been acquired implicitly mainly (as in untutored second language learning) are less vulnerable than more explicitly learned languages. No evidence exists on this at the moment. One problem is that it is not easy or even possible to define exactly which part of an individual's language has been acquired implicitly or explicitly. The implicit/explicit distinction can also account for the differences found with respect to decline of lexical skills vs. morpho-syntactic skills. Lexical knowledge is basically explicit knowledge in Paradis's view, while morpho-syntactic knowledge may be explicit or implicit. The vulnerability of lexical knowledge results from its explicit character.

The number of studies on foreign/second-language proficiency and its decline in the elderly is remarkably small. Weltens' (1989) review of the literature on foreign-language attrition shows that attention has merely been focused on age groups under 25, especially former secondary school pupils and university students. Empirical data on foreign/second-language proficiency in the elderly are available from several studies by Clyne (1977, 1982) and from the investigation by Bahrick (1984).

Clyne's work on language loss and language maintenance in Dutch and German migrants in Australia has been pioneering in this respect. He recorded spontaneous speech in English from 200 postwar Dutch migrants and their children and 600 German-English bilinguals (half of them migrants, the other half Australian-born), and analyzed the pattern of switching and interference in their respective languages. One of the outcomes of his research was that a number of elderly migrants tended to become less fluent in the second language, while the number of transfers and switches into the first language increased (1982: 27). Clyne lists a number of explanations for this 'reversion' to the first language. The most likely explanation is the change in social setting, retirement, the absence of children, and the decreased socio-economic value of English; but 'the phenomena described are not restricted to the retired or those whose children live away from home. They are even found in elderly migrants active in the work force who are married to English speakers' (Clyne, 1977: 50).

The most extensive study in the field of foreign-language attrition is undoubtedly Bahrick's (1984) study. In this study the retention of Spanish learned in school was tested throughout a 50-year period for 733 individuals. Each individual was tested on a large number of aspects of language proficiency. The data show that memory curves for Spanish decline exponentially for the first three to six years of the retention interval. After that retention remains stable for periods of up to 30 years. Then the memory curves show what Bahrick calls a 'final decline' (1984: 1).

For the purpose of this chapter we want to look more closely at the oldest informants in Bahrick's study who were tested 50 years (on average) after the completion of the acquisition process (group 8). In the analyses these subjects show a remarkable drop in their scores when compared to younger groups, in particular with regard to grammar recognition, word-order, reading comprehension, Spanish-English and English-Spanish vocabulary recall. No decline was found for grammar recall, idiom recall, Spanish-English and English-Spanish vocabulary recognition. Bahrick himself refrains from speculating about possible explanations for the different scores in group 8 in his study. In his comments on Bahrick's study Neisser (1984: 34) says: 'It is too early to tell whether this downturn is universal or particular; whether it is an age effect, a cohort effect, a time-in-storage effect, or a result of some other factor yet unknown'. Information about age is not provided in Bahrick's study, but a post-training interval of 50 years suggests that these subjects are at least 65 years old, so there is some ground for assuming an age effect or a cohort effect. Although Bahrick wanted to investigate the amount of rehearsal needed to maintain a particular level of performance, he failed to accomplish this goal because his informants rehearsed so little that no correlations could be found between retention and rehearsal variables. In our study we were not interested in the amount of knowledge forgotten due to a long period of non-use, but in the interaction between foreign-language proficiency and age in cases where rehearsal actually did take place.

Another study that looked at the retention of *foreign* language skills is one by de Bot and Lintsen (1986) on German and French in the Netherlands. It was part of the project by Lintsen reported on in Chapter 4. It should be remembered that this study looked at language skills in highly educated, independently living, healthy men. The main purpose of this study was to investigate to what extent the data on language proficiency in the elderly support Bahrick's findings. The data for German as a foreign language show that the elderly informants (mean age 75) made slightly more grammatical and lexical errors in spontaneous speech. For verbal fluency the elderly outperformed the younger group on two out of three letters, and their error rates were also lower. No differences between age groups were found on a range of other measures. As in many other studies on language attrition, a self-evaluation instrument was used to study reported change over time. The participants had to rate their proficiency on a number of can-do statements ('Conversing with friends on an every day topic') for three moments in their lives: at the end of secondary education; at the peak of the command of the foreign language; and now. Interestingly, there was a clear pattern for improvement after school and hardly any change between 'peak' and 'now' . This is in clear contrast with the findings in the language attrition literature of a general feeling of having lost the language over time. These data also contrast with Bahrick's findings. Although the informants are at least the same age as Bahrick's informants (group 8), there are important differences in initial training level and in the amount of rehearsal. In Bahrick's study there were 33 subjects in group 8, most of them (27) with a training level of 2 to 4, i.e. two to four years of high-school Spanish instruction or two to four one-semester college courses or combinations of high school and college courses (one year high school = one term or semester in college). So the initial training level of Bahrick's informants was not very high. The remaining six subjects had a training level comparable to that of our informants: three to six years of foreign-language instruction. Bahrick suggests that the amount of loss is independent of the initiate level of training. The Dutch data could be explained by postulating that higher initial levels of training suffer less attrition, both in relative and in absolute terms.

Another difference is the amount of rehearsal. The informants in the Dutch study did not stop using the foreign language after the acquisition period. Significant differences between the (self-reported) knowledge of the foreign language at the end of secondary school and the peak of their command indicate that the informants had additional contact with the foreign language. Craik *et al*. (1977, 1982) cite a number of studies to show that memory performance in the elderly tends to remain fairly stable for tasks that are ecologically valid, i.e. tasks that test the retention of knowledge that has been acquired and maintained in meaningful activities. The use of foreign languages was a meaningful activity for the participants in the Dutch study, which may explain the retention found.

In the USA the focus has been on English and Spanish as the main languages of multilinguals. Rosselli *et al.* (1999) compared performance of an English monolingual group and a Spanish-English bilingual group on a number of tests, including verbal fluency, sentence repetition, and picture description. In both groups subjects' ages range from 55 to 84. The monolinguals showed higher scores on semantic verbal fluency than the bilinguals, while the bilinguals had a higher number of connected words in spontaneous speech. Within the bilingual subjects group higher number of words in the English picture description test were found. Since the groups were very small (seven and eight subjects), no effects of age could be measured. Also the range of the subjects ages was large, making it difficult to see such results as giving useful information about elderly in different age ranges. A much larger study is the one by Acevado *et al.* (2000) on verbal fluency norms in Spanish and English speakers over 50 years of age. The results show that age, education and gender are the most important factors predicting scores on both groups regardless of primary language. The two groups had similar scores for animal and fruit fluency, while the English group scored higher on the vegetables category.

So far the effect of structural differences between languages has not been studied much. Kempler *et al.* (1998) compared performance on a semantic verbal fluency task in a group of elderly subjects including Chinese, Hispanic and Vietnamese immigrants as well as white and Afro-American English speakers. In this study, there were differences for age and education, but here we want to focus on the differences between ethnic groups. Language differences appear to play a major role: The Vietnamese subjects produced many more animal names than the Spanish subjects. This is attributed to the fact that in Vietnamese, animal names are short (mostly one syllable) while in Spanish animal names are longer. This points to one of the problems in comparing data between languages: the same test may lead to different scores within the same individual because of differences between the linguistic systems.

All in all the research we have does not seem to support Paradis's prediction of second language attrition with aging, though it should be kept in mind that the research that has been done was not set up to test the specific predictions of his theory.

Multilingualism and Dementia

Again, the number of studies on multilingualism and dementia is very small, and most of them are concerned with variants of the verbal fluency task and various types of code-switching.

De Picciotto and Friedland (2001) investigated verbal fluency abilities in healthy and demented English-Afrikaans bilinguals. In contrast to most research in verbal fluency and aging, no effect of aging was found for the healthy bilinguals when they were tested in their bilingual mode, i.e. when they were allowed to use both languages. Pattern of use of the languages had no effect on the fluency data.

There is some research in code-switching (CS) and dementia, though it is often linked to forms of aphasia. Until the mid-1980s the trend was to discuss language problems in bilinguals within the bilingual aphasia framework (e.g. Albert & Obler 1978, who briefly refer to two cases of involuntary code-switching in patients with senile dementia). The literature on code-switching and dementia is discussed by Friedland and Miller (1999). The research focuses on two main issues: language choice and language separation (Ludérus, 1995). The distinction between these two issues is not always properly made and they may show overlap, and in cases of CS in conversations it is not always exactly clear what causes the switch. There is anecdotal evidence of a higher incidence of CS in dementia patients, but the research done is not in all aspects convincing. Levels of proficiency of the patients and information on switching behavior before the onset of cognitive decline are more often than not absent, as is information on patterns of CS in the community the patients come from. Also some CS is more appropriate than simple counts can tell, e.g. in settings in which multilinguals play a role or in which the language to be used is unclear (Perecman, 1984). Friedland and Miller make a plea for using conversational analysis as a better approach, because it is better able to define to what extent CS is or is not appropriate in a given situation. At the same time they have to admit that such analyses do not tell us much more on the mechanisms that govern CS, and in particular with dementia patients guessing for motives is hazardous. For example, what may be perceived as inappropriate CS for healthy speakers may be perceived as very appropriate by patients, when they interpret the situation differently. This is supported by Hyltenstam's (1995) analysis of cases of code-switching reported in the literature. He also notes that on the basis of the information given on the older (pre-1960s) cases in the literature it is hard to say to what extent code-switching was a part of normal language use of the patients. His analysis shows that it is not always the case that speakers with dementia have more problems keeping their languages apart and choosing the right language in conversations: 'In conclusion, it is probably safe to say that neither code-switching problems nor language choice problems are necessary consequences of all stages of deterioration in dementia for bilingual speakers.' On the basis of data from patients they tested, Hyltenstam makes the suggestion that a second language learned in adulthood is 'probably more affected by the limited processing capacity which is a typical effect of dementia, so that the patients would generally – partly or totally – revert to their first language when interacting with speakers of their first language, but not the other way around' (Hyltenstam, 1995: 319).

From the literature of the cases mentioned, the conclusion is that there does not seem to be a relation between severity of dementia and amount of CS, while there is an effect of level of proficiency in the sense that more CS takes place from the dominant language into the non-dominant language than in the other direction. This has been found in many studies of healthy speakers too. It is obvious that general finding of lack of control and disinhibition, which is normally seen as characteristic for dementia patients, does not simply lead to lack of control over languages in conversations. Van de Ven (1987) describes the case of an 81-year-old multilingual who had a stroke leading to right hemisphere brain damage, and who after the stroke showed extensive language switching between Dutch, Italian and English. Another interesting aspect of this case is that he never finished primary education and acquired all of his foreign languages working as an acrobat in a circus touring in various European countries, and that he was basically illiterate, which turned out to be a problem when administering the Bilingual Aphasia Test (BAT). He was tested with parts of the BAT and showed a pattern of aphasia with serious production problems and word-finding problems in particular. His score on the Short Portable Mental Status Questionnaire (SPMSQ) was 3 out of 30 which suggest serious cognitive decline. When tested in Dutch some switching to Italian and English occurred. When tested in Italian, probably his best second language, he had serious problems staying in that language, mixing in words and morphemes from Dutch all the time. His case is similar to the one reported by Perecman (1984), which also showed patterns of code-switching due to both confusion about the language required in the testing setting, and an inability to keep the two languages apart. As Kemper *et al.* (1995) and various other authors have argued, loss of control, and in particular disinhibition, are among the more prominent characteristics of various forms of dementia. In the cases reported on by Van de Ven and Perecman, inability to block the inappropriate language is probably the best explanation for the findings. The problem with the case described by Van de Ven is that the effects of general cognitive decline as a result of global brain degeneration, and the impact of the more local impact of the stroke interact: according to his spouse, the switching between languages only began after the stroke. At the same time there is only one other case of involuntary switching with right/non-dominant hemisphere mentioned in the literature (Gloning & Gloning, 1965, case 4).

One of the few longitudinal studies on dementia in multilinguals was carried out by Ludérus (1995). She presents three cases of women who grew up in a German-speaking environment and moved to the Netherlands. In those patients there was CS from German, their dominant language, into Dutch, but far less in the other direction. Her patients were able to intentionally switch languages, e.g. in quotations from the other language, so the switching mechanism as such was still there, but she also mentions that the language choice problems may be (partly) caused by confusion and inadequate interpretation of the conversational setting. Because the patients appear to be able to use both languages at other occasions, Ludérus concludes 'that it is not a language separation problem that underlies the inappropriate (base-) language use, but instead a language choice problem' (p. 124).

The test-setting may also be a source of confusion with respect to the language to be used. This is clearly the case with the patient in the study by Perecman (1984) mentioned earlier. Analyses of her test sessions showed that the two testers, who were pretending to be monolingual speakers of the two languages tested, were constantly interacting between them about what to do next, so creating confusion about the language to be used. The translation behavior of the patient was at first interpreted as some sort of compulsive drive to translate spontaneously, therefore, was in fact adequate from the perspective of the patient: two languages were used and thus it was better to repeat what was said in the other language. The patients tested by Ludérus were not interrupted or corrected when they switched to the other language, which may have created the impression that the use of those two languages was in fact adequate.

Language Choice in Production

The language choice problems do not need to be caused by a deficit in the selection mechanisms themselves. Memory problems and reduced processing resources make language use more effortful and may therefore lead to the selection of whatever words and rules that can be found in time. In language production lexical elements and morpho-syntactic procedures have to be selected and activated under enormous time constraints, often less than 200 ms, and therefore 'language' as a selection criterion may be overruled by other constraints (see de Bot, 1998, 2004). During those laborious word-finding processes, words from the other language may present themselves as alternatives. Hyltenstam and Stroud (1989) observed that their patient showed more intra-sentential code-switching when the other language had been used shortly before by the interlocutor. Use of a language increases its level of activation and accordingly the chance of elements of that language to be selected. Depending on when and how well a language is learned in the past, it will have some sort of default level of activation (de Bot & Schreuder, 1993). In most bilinguals, one of the languages will clearly be the dominant one, quite often the one acquired in primary socialization and before puberty. The typical finding in research on code-switching is that the amount of code-switching from the dominant language into the non-dominant language is larger than in the opposite direction. This is also found in most cases of bilingual dementia patients. In the analysis of language behavior in bilingual patients, conversational patterns of code-switching have to be taken into account. There is nothing pathological about code-switching when that is the normal mode in the community. It is rather the peculiarity of a testing setting in which languages all of a sudden have to be strictly separate that is unusual and may therefore lead to disorientation.

For the study of language and dementia in bilinguals, there are different layers in the analysis of the language problems. As we have argued in Chapter 5, there are general problems in working memory/processing resources and attentional processes. This leads to problems of disorientation and disengagement, which will have an effect on testing conditions and results. The second layer is formed by the specific language problems that are the result of the resources and attention problems. We have argued that those problems have an impact on basically all subprocesses of language production and perception, though more automatized lower level skills such as sentence formation and articulation will be affected less than higher level non-automatized skills such as interpretation of the discourse setting, maintenance of the discourse record and interpretation of indirect meanings. The next layer is about problems that have to do with the multiple languages in bilingual patients. The general processing problems will have an impact on choosing the right language (or languages, when code-switching is the norm) in a given situation. It has been argued that in different subprocesses of language production there are potential 'switching sites' (de Bot, 2001). These switching sites often coincide with the sites where parts of language have to be stored or buffered before final processing (see Chapter 5). At these sites elements from the inappropriate language may be selected and stored for processing. One of the big debates in bilingual processing is whether bilinguals activate their languages in parallel or that the choice to use one language only is taken at an early stage with the exclusion or inhibition of the other language (Gollan & Kroll, 2000). In settings in which both languages are likely to play a role, parallel activation is more likely (cf. van Heuven, 2000). This means that code-switching can take place very easily at different points in the process and at each site the inappropriate language has to be inhibited. A reduced capacity to inhibit the other language may well be one of the explanations for the code-switching behavior in demented patients.

Modeling Language and Aging in Multilinguals

As indicated in Chapter 5 there are a number interacting variables and resources that make up the developing language system. Here we will focus on how multilingualism has an impact on these variables and resources.

Neurophysiological changes

Following Paradis's model of the neurolinguistics of multilingualism, we assume that there are no specific components in the brain for handling multilingualism as compared to monolingualism. Multilinguals use the same components and their neural substrates as monolinguals, but they may be using them in different ways. For example, lower levels of proficiency may lead to more extensive use of pragmatic strategies that are assumed to be located in the non-dominant hemisphere. Accordingly, specific local changes in the brain may have a differential impact on different components and this may show in different patterns of language use. The neuro-part is beyond the scope of the present book and we will not dwell on this any further, though there clearly is a need for research on the impact of neurophysiological changes on language in aging and dementia.

Reduction of resource capacity

Working memory has been discussed as one of the main components of the processing system that may be affected by aging. As we discussed in Chapter 5, language proficiency and working memory capacity may interact (Miyake & Friedman, 1999): higher levels of proficiency lead to more effective coding of information in working memory. Whether that means that a decline in working memory capacity has a differential effect on the first vs. a second or third language is unclear. Speed of processing is the other component in resource capacity. It is a general finding that even for advanced speakers of a second language, speed of processing in the second language, as measured in reaction time experiments, is lower than in their L1 (Woutersen, 1997). If this speed further decreases, processing of speech may become too slow for normal communication. No research on the interaction between aging and processing speed in L1 and L2 has been done so far.

Stereotypes of behavior towards the elderly

One important aspect is the old and young people's belief about intergenerational communication. There are common beliefs about cultural differences on this, and in particular on the status of old age in different cultures. Data by Williams *et al.* (1997) undermine such general beliefs, in particular that Eastern societies value old age more than Western societies. In some societies more negative attitudes were found, and the variability among Eastern cultures was such that a simple East/West distinction becomes obsolete. There may be one aspect of multilingualism in the elderly that could have positive effects on stereotype behavior: in many societies the ability to speak more languages has prestige, and elderly people who have a good command of one or more foreign languages may be seen more positively. So in that sense, multilingualism and the actual showing of proficiency in other languages may have a positive effect on how elderly people are seen and accordingly treated.

Changes in interaction with elderly people

The changes in interaction patterns with elderly people as such may not be influenced by the fact that there is one or more language. Still, in many situations, elderly people may end up in a nursing situation in which their language is not the normal one and where actually no one speaks that language (see Overberg, 1984 on elderly Dutch migrants in Australia). In most western-European countries large sections of the population have a migrant background, and the then 'guestworkers' are now getting older, and due to various reasons have a higher chance of developing cognitive decline with aging. This means that the proportion of elderly people with a allochtonous background in institutions that provide health care and nursing homes will increase dramatically over the next decade. So far the awareness of these problems appears to be very low in most countries and few initiatives have been taken to provide adequate care for these groups. Elderly people in institutions who have no one to talk to are typically prone to developing depression and withdrawal symptoms and their language and interaction skills will deteriorate accordingly.

Decline of language skills and other behavioral changes

So far there is little research to show that multilinguals are more likely to develop cognitive and linguistic decline as compared to monolinguals. One would expect that knowledge of more than one language, in particular when the languages are related and there is overlap between the languages with respect to grammar and lexicon, will actually act as a buffer in decline, because the list of words and ways of expression is larger and there is more to choose from. There may actually be decline in knowledge and skills but due to the buffer it will show only later in the process. In fact, there is as yet little evidence showing decline in second language skills in the elderly. Of course this relates to what the definition of proficiency is. Is it the knowledge of grammatical rules and lexical items in a test, or the ability to communicate in the other language? The self-evaluation data reported on by de Bot and Lintsen (1986) suggest that the elderly men they studied feel that they have not lost the language at all, which may reflect their ability to do relevant activities, like reading in a foreign language, or interact with speakers of that language, rather than the list of rules and words they know.

Why Test Different Languages?

As Paradis (2004) has argued, there is no basis for postulating different processing mechanisms or neurophysiological structures that are specific for multilingual vs. monolingual processing. What may differ is the extent to which multilinguals make use of different mechanisms and resources. It is not clear to what extent specific changes on all levels (neurophysiological, functional, social) may lead to differential decline of language with aging and dementia. As the study of bilingual aphasia has shown (Albert & Obler, 1978; Paradis, 1993, 2004), all sorts of patterns of decline and recovery have been found. Therefore, a full picture of the language skills of an individual can only be found when he or she is tested in all the languages that had once been acquired. Though the normal pattern will be that the first language and the most frequently used language recover best and are best retained, it is not impossible that that language, which may also be the language of daily use, is affected more than other languages. In such a case the other languages may provide opportunities for communication and treatment. Not testing other languages, and not being aware of the dangers of testing in the dominant language only, may lead to misdiagnosis in elderly patients and patients with aphasia (Dronkers *et al.*, 1995). This issue will be taken up in the study of African-Americans reported on in Chapter 7.

Testing Language in Aging Minority Populations

Neuropsychological testing in minority groups is complicated by a number of factors. The first is that minority groups may simply not make use of health services even if they are provided for free. Harris (1999) reports on the under use of speech-language pathology services for

African-Americans. The second is that while culture and ethnicity are easily taken as a main independent variable, they are in fact difficult to define and accordingly, to measure in a valid way. Group membership is often difficult to establish, boundaries between groups are often blurred and constantly changing. Also differences on crucial variables may be larger within the group than between groups, in particular when the group is large and varied in its history of migration or acculturation in mainstream society (Suzuki & Valencia 1997).

The Use of Tests in Multilingual and Multi-ethnic Populations

A serious problem in assessing cognitive decline in multilingual and multi-ethnic populations, in particular when part of the population has a low level of education, is the use of adequate tests. Norms for the population in a given country may not be adequate for minority groups as McCurry *et al.* (2001) show for a group of healthy Japanese-Americans. Marien *et al.* (1998) compared various other language versions of the Boston Naming Test, and found few cultural differences, but her sample was restricted to Western societies. Related to this is the problem of matching neuropsychological tests across languages. Obviously, simple translations may lead to specific biases based on the original language text, and specific measures need to be taken to make different language versions of tests comparable in what they measure. Mungas *et al.* (2000) used Item Response Theory (IRT) to develop matched English/Spanish forms of a neuropsychological test. Using IRT, reasonably good matches between scales in the two languages could be achieved. The main advantage is that IRT can help to eliminate linguistically biased items. The psychometric characteristics of various language versions of tests need to be established before it can be claimed that they measure the same constructs in different languages. That such translation problems occur is shown in a study by McDowell *et al.* (1997) who compare the quality of a modified version of the Mini-Mental State Exam (MMSE) in English-speaking and French-speaking populations in Canada. The results showed that the adapted version of the test produced inconsistencies between the two language groups.

Another approach to testing cognitive decline is the use of learning tests. In such tests subjects have to learn new verbal items and are requested to recall them at a later stage. They have been shown to be highly sensitive, but as Gonzales *et al.* (2001) show, they may be less appropriate for minority groups. The authors looked specifically at older Spanish- and English-speaking people in the USA in order to develop cut-off points for specific groups. The tests appeared to correlate well with the MMSE. No major differences were found between the two language groups, suggesting that this approach may be a valid one in comparing across ethnic groups.

Borson *et al.* (1999) propose a simple test, the Clock Drawing Test as an alternative for standard measures like MMSE and CASI. It is less dependent on language skills, test-experience and education. The test appears to discriminate between dementia/non-dementia about as reliably as the standard measures but requires no experienced testers of bilingual interpreters to administer.

Cross-cultural Differences in Testing

Cross-cultural differences are important as factors to take into account when testing for cognitive decline. One of the issues here is to what extent pervasive childhood cultural experiences continue to influence processing at later stages. Park *et al.* (1999) argue that there is evidence for fundamental differences in information processing between East Asians and western Europeans. While the former are biased to process information in a holistic, contextual fashion, the latter use a more analytic, feature-based style. Such differences may be so pervasive that they have an impact on basic cognitive operations. Park *et al.* argue that due to cognitive decline with aging as a universal tendency, these differences are likely to become smaller, resulting in more similarity in cognitive functioning in late adulthood than in young adulthood. Data to support this view are still missing, but the issues are clearly relevant and call for culture-invariant measures of processing, though that may be fundamentally impossible if basic mechanisms are as different as the authors claim. Obviously, the whole area of cross-cultural aspects of aging needs to be developed further to make comparisons valid.

Yano *et al.* (2000) tested a group of 3734 Japanese American men aged 71–93 in Hawaii. The aim was to test the effect of the number of years spent in Japan during childhood on cognitive test performance, and to test the role of the language used in testing. The data show that there is an inverse relation between scores on cognitive tests and number of years spent in Japan in middle childhood, irrespective of age, education, acculturation and level of proficiency in Japanese. When the groups were split up according to preferred language of testing, it turned out that for the men tested in English the relationship between years in Japan and cognitive performance was negative while it was positive for those tested in Japanese. This is remarkable given the fact that the subjects could choose the language of testing. Apparently the impact of the years in Japan went deeper than the subjects themselves were aware of. As the authors conclude: 'To assess cognitive test performance in older people, it is of prime importance to use the most optimal language for testing, usually the subject's native language' (p. 204)

One of the consistent findings over the years is that many normal (i.e. cognitively non-impaired) ethnic minority subjects in the USA have lower scores than their Anglo-American counterparts, which leads to high rates of misclassification. In his discussion of cultural and ethnic differences in neuropsychological assessment Gasquoine (1999) argues that one solution, race-norming ('using separate norms for different cultural and ethnic groups', p. 376) is controversial, easily leading to difficult discussions on race superiority issues. Rather than taking ethnicity as a given characteristic, it is argued that culture and ethnicity as independent variables should be replaced by measurable psychological and socio-economic dimensions that characterize such groups. Relevant variables include: education, language skills in L1 and L2, acculturation and socio-economic status. Similar trends can be found in research in education with minority groups. For example, Driessen *et al.* (2002) analyzed a large data set of performance measures of children in primary education in the Netherlands. While they included information about ethnic origin, their data show that the lower scores of many migrant children are in fact not explained by ethnic origin, but employment status of parents, and accordingly the group of children at risk is not restricted to migrant groups (in which unemployment is high) but includes indigenous children as well.

Test-bias, the risk of deviant test scores because of specific group characteristics is very difficult to avoid. Groups may differ in level of literacy, level of education and experience in doing tests. A good (or bad) example is the Spanish language and (Puerto-Rican) culture adaptation of the Wechsler Adult Intelligence scales (WAIS). According to Melendez (1994) the changes lead to an overestimation of IQs by more than a standard deviation. Gasquoine (1999) discusses some other problems in the use of various tests with the Hispanic group in the USA. He shows that the group in itself is highly heterogeneous, that there are many flaws in the adapted versions of tests (and even competing versions of the same test), that the group varies with respect to level of fluency in English and in particular with respect to level of education. Level of education is normally defined as the number of years in education, making the implicit, but clearly wrong assumption that quality of education for different groups is similar. Education is typically highly correlated with socio-economic status (SES). Finally degree and level of poverty may have an impact independent of the other factors. Prolonged poverty with the ensuing problems of nutrition, contact with schools and parental involvement is likely to have a deeper effect than temporary poverty. Gasquoine (2001) reviews the neuropsychological research on Hispanic Americans thereby showing some of the most pervasive problems in that research. The research discussed appears to cover a very wide range of groups who's only common trait seems to be the fact that they speak more or less the same language. The variation in level of education, degree of acculturation (i.e. number of years in the USA), degree of fluency in English and SES is huge, and accordingly developing one adapted version of standard tests for this whole group seems unwarranted.

The discussion on the adaptation of tests sometimes seems to be flawed towards avoiding cultural bias. This may blur the perspective on the aim of many of the tests, i.e. to assess differences. While there can be discussion on the cultural fairness of translations of widely used measures, the ultimate test is whether they adequately discriminate between pathology and non-pathology. A good example is the MMSE which has been translated in Spanish. Tausig *et al.* (1992) show that the test adequately discriminates between demented and non-demented speakers of Spanish.

It may not be enough to have translated versions of the tests. There may be grounds to stratify within specific groups by age, education and degree of bilingualism and acculturation (Gasquoine, 2001). The latter two are essential for choosing the language or languages of testing. Having a Spanish-speaking background does not necessarily imply that Spanish is also the most adequate language for the assessment (Artiola I Fotuny *et al.* 1998). It could be argued that the assessment should be done on both languages (English and Spanish), since the literature on decline due to local or global brain damage has shown that the language that is best retained need not always be the language learnt first or best or the language commonly spoken before the onset of the decline. Also, we basically do not know what language or languages are most easily sustained or restored.

Language in Autobiographical Memory

The arguments for the use of the right language in testing are further supported by the work of Schrauf (2000). He discusses the autobiographical memory of bilinguals by looking at research from experimental psychology and psychoanalysis. He concludes that 'memory retrieval for events from childhood and youth (in the country of origin) are more numerous, more detailed and more emotionally marked when remembering is done in the first language ('mother-tongue hypothesis') rather than in the second language' (p. 387). The explanation given for this is that there is encoding specificity which includes languages and state-dependent learning. For testing of memory in multilingual elderly the implication is that the language used in testing may have an impact on more recent or more distant memories, and that test batteries testing memory should take this into account.

In psycho-analytic studies various types of language related/code-switching induced memories have been witnessed. The language may actually serve to repress or inhibit specific painful memories:

> I'm afraid. I don't want to talk German. I have the feeling that in talking German I shall have to remember something that I wanted to forget. (From Greenson, 1950, cited by Schrauf, 2000)

Reference is made to the literature on multiple selves that may be formed by and mediated by different languages. Schmid (2003) reports similar comments from elderly Jewish people who fled Germany in the 1930s and for whom the language is still related to what they had to go through in those years.

Summary

The main aim of this chapter is to argue for more attention to multiple languages in elderly people in diagnosis and treatment. Even though the majority of the population in most countries, even the USA, uses more than one language (which includes dialects and varieties of standard languages) the medical profession shows a strong monolingual bias in its approach. There are now quite a few instruments that allow for testing skills in various languages, and more use should be made of them. We are not arguing that using different languages will inevitably lead to better diagnosis and treatment, but we do argue for the perspective of multiple languages as assets rather than as disadvantages. With different languages come different cultures. As with monolingualism, the assumption of mono-culturalism in any society is wrong, and that applies to the elderly population as much as it does for other populations.

A dynamic systems approach can be instrumental in laying out the interactions between and within multilingual systems. It provides a framework for discussion of various aspects of language and aging in multilingual societies and individuals by linking components of the cognitive system with components from the social environment that all appear to interact in the larger multilingual systems as it develops.

Chapter 7

Bilingual Aging in Older African-Americans

Theoretically, the study explores the impact of bilingualism on aging, when bilingualism is situated within a Dynamic Systems perspective. Our interest in bilingualism in Dynamic Systems is part of a general theoretical interest in an exploration of the potential impact of resource utilization in aging particularly in bilingual elderly persons.

The aim of this chapter is to examine issues about language and aging in African-American communities in the United States. The rapid growth in the older African-Americans, and their under-representation in aging research, relative low levels of education which increases their susceptibility to late-life dementias (Ganguli & Ratcliff 1996) are powerful enough arguments for conducting research in language and dementia within African-American communities.

Demographically, the African-American population is projected to grow at a rate estimated at 20% faster than the European American one (US Census Bureau, 2000). In spite of the projected demographic increase African-Americans are heavily under-represented in language and aging research relative to other ethnic minorities in the United States (Lichtenberg, 1998; Hendrie *et al.*, 1993; Hendrie *et al.*, 1995). Health oriented research in the United States in ethnic minorities, including African-Americans, has tended to focus on high visibility diseases such as asthma, diabetes, hypertension, cardiovascular diseases, and infant mortality, and has not focused on cognitive impairment as a consequence of aging or dementia. Research into language in African-Americans is thus a relatively new area, and this chapter pioneers it. Although there has been a considerable amount of research on African-Americans with some of it focusing on dementia in African-Americans (Gurland, 1996; Hendrie *et al.*, 1993), the research has lacked a bilingual thrust (Lichtenberg, 1998; Hendrie *et al.*, 1995). The research reported in this chapter explores the effects of aging, education, cognitive and physical status on African-Americans.

A large majority of research subjects in aging research tend to be white, educated and middle-class Americans. The homogeneity of the research subjects is unfortunate because it shapes our understanding of disease etiology. For example, connections between diabetes, stroke and dementia, which could easily have eluded researchers for a long period of time, are becoming apparent through studies into disease conditions in ethnically diverse populations such as Latinos and African-Americans. Diabetes and hypertension are widely prevalent in ethnic minorities and it is increasingly becoming apparent that they constitute high risk factors for dementia (Haan *et al.*, 2003). Connections between diabetes, high blood pressure, stroke. etc. are easier to make when the research is focused on ethnic minorities such as African-Americans and Latinos because of the high incidence of diabetes (some of which is uncontrolled), and hypertension in such ethnic minorities. The inclusion of ethnic minorities is therefore necessary not only because it is fair to do so but for scientific reasons as well. A focus on ethnic minorities, however, raises important issues relating to bilingualism and aging.

Specific Problems Relating to Research in Language and Aging with African-Americans and Other Ethnic Minorities

The inclusion of African-Americans and other ethnic minorities – although socially and scientifically justifiable – poses specific challenges both of a linguistic and cultural nature which have to be addressed, if the results are to be valid. In the following section we describe the challenges and outline the strategies we adopted to overcome them. A majority of African-Americans speak one version or other of African-American Vernacular (AAV) (also variously referred to as Ebonics, Black English, African-American English, African-American Language). Smitherman (1977, 2000) places the figure of African-Americans who speak a variety of AAV or other as high as 90%, while an earlier study (Dillard, 1972) placed the figure relatively lower at 80%. Smitherman's estimate is higher than that of Dillard's because she is using a much broader conceptualization of AAV than Dillard. Her conceptualization of AAV includes both grammatical structures and rhetorical strategies while Dillard restricts his notion of AAV to grammatical structures only. In spite of this difference in the estimates made by Dillard and Smitherman, we can safely claim that a majority of African-Americans speak AAV in addition to Standard American English (SAE). Because African-Americans speak AAV and SAE they can be categorized as bidialectal. In this book, bidialectalism is treated as a subcategory of bilingualism, hence the bilingualism in the title of this chapter. Because bidialectalism is seen here as a subtype of bilingualism this chapter focuses on the impact of aging in older bilingual African-Americans.

Current research which has examined the interaction between clinical conditions and AAV has by and large been restricted to children and aphasics (Seymour, 1986, 1991; Ulatowska *et al.*, 2000). There are no aging studies that we are aware of which have systematically examined African-American bilingualism and aging. To date most of the research on AAV has focused on the historical origins, structural, educational aspects of AAV (Smitherman, 1981, 1994; Spears, 1999, 2002). This study focuses on people who self-select as African-Americans speaking AAV. This is an important issue because AAV is also spoken as a second language by other ethnicities (Alim, 2003; Brice, 2002).

Although most African-Americans are bilingual speaking one version or other of AAV and SAE, unfortunately most neuropsychological assessment instruments are normed using white monolingual middle-class Americans and may therefore not necessarily be valid when extended to bilingual African-Americans. Research on the language patterns of African-Americans has demonstrated the existence of linguistic and discourse patterns that are substantially different from those of white mainstream America. These structural features of AAV have to be taken into account when African-Americans are being assessed neuropsychologically (Smitherman, 1994; Baugh, 1999, 2003).

AAV and the Use of Screening Instruments

The linguistic problems of simply applying neuropsychological instruments designed with speakers of SAE in mind is easily illustrated when we focus on an extensively used neuropsychological assessment widely used in aging research: the Mini-Mental State Examination (MMSE), (Folstein *et al.*, 1975). When the MMSE is being used participants are instructed to write 'a sentence of their choice which contains a subject and a verb'. Linguistically, the instructions are to 'produce' a sentence which contains a 'subject' and 'verb' although appropriate for SAE are inappropriate when used with AAV in mind. In many syntactic environments AAV sentences do not necessarily always have to contain verbs for them to be regarded as grammatical. For example, in the speech of a cognitively intact 79-year-old woman reporting 10 and half years of education in our Detroit project produced the following sentences which are grammatical according to AAV rules but did not contain verbs.

(1) She not here today.
(2) The dog in the chair.

Even when verbs are supplied their presence may be variable. For example, the suppliance of a copula in AAV is known to be variable.

According to Smitherman (2000), the variability in verb production, particularly the copula, is a result of a complex interaction of linguistic and semantic factors, as the following list of sentences by an 88-year-old cognitively intact woman reporting six years of formal education illustrator in the following sentences:

(1) The dog in the yard.
(2) The chair is in the doctor's office.
(3) The drawer is open in the kitchen cabinet.
(4) The red car in the garage.

In some cases memorable sentences which do indeed contain 'subjects' and 'verbs' are produced as the 83-year-old woman reporting three years of education says:

(7) I've got to go to the bathroom!

There are also discourse features of AAV such as topic association, circumlocutory style, and narrativizing which may be inaccurately construed as indices of dementia and functional impairment rather than discourse styles typical of African-American speech. Knowledge of African-American discourse 'genres' is useful when making judgments about the quality of the discourse, and trying to determine whether the discourse is impaired or not. Attuning to the narrativizing style of African-Americans is necessary even in the administration of questionnaires and neuropsychological protocols. For example, an 84-year-old woman when asked whether she does her own shopping as part of the Assessment of Activities of Daily Living (ADL), (Katz *et al.*, 1963) to evaluate her functional abilities talks about her personal experiences with shopping: a type of response which might be construed as 'off-target' speech, but is clearly a rhetorical style appropriate to African-American discourse communities.

There are also further problems with the use of the 'idiom' typically used when administering the MMSE. For example, terms such as 'sentences' predicate upon a literacy view of language are at variance with that of communities with relatively low degrees of formal literacy. For example, in the MMSE African-American respondents found the question that they should spell the word 'world' backwards and still be denied permission to write it down counter intuitive and they frequently asserted that the question was 'crazy'. The participants also closely associated the tasks with school: as one informant put it, 'you talking school now not health'. Because of their relatively low degrees of education some of the respondents might not be 'test wise'. 'Test wiseness' is construed here to refer to the ability to respond speedily and accurately during neuropsychological assessment (Neill,

2001). African-Americans, like many other cultures, do not necessarily value speed, a trait which is highly valued in neuropsychological assessment. In such cultures speed may be construed as recklessness. Test-wiseness may also have to do with problems in using decontextualized language.

Experience from the administration of the MMSE to populations with relatively limited formal education has shown that items such as 'arithmetic' and 'spelling words backwards' may not be ecologically valid. That the use of a wrong variety of language may lead to a serious misdiagnosis is not a purely theoretical possibility. Dronkers _et al._ (1986) showed that errors in the standard variety of English are actually acceptable in Hawaii Creole English.

Another challenge which bilingual neuropsychological assessment is faced with in assessing bilingual African-Americans is how to design an assessment protocol in which items are equivalent in AAV and SAE. In this chapter this requires designing neuropsychological instruments of equivalent levels of difficulty between AAV and SAE.

A challenge which has to be addressed when seeking to include ethnic minorities, particularly African-Americans in aging and dementia research and indeed in most medical research is the fact that most older African-Americans, are skeptical of medical research, because African-Americans have reported histories of being abused by medical research. Reluctance to participate might have been a result of the fact that dementia is not a high visibility disease, unlike diabetes and hypertension in African-American communities. In order to overcome the recruitment problem in aging research dementia was presented discursively as one possible outcome of uncontrolled 'diabetes', 'hypertension', 'untreated injuries', and excessive alcoholism' and repeated strokes. Rhetorically Alzheimer's disease was presented as the main protagonist of dementia in older persons.

The recruitment targeted specific communities in Detroit, Michigan, and did not rely on clinical and hospital referrals. It was necessary to design a community based strategy rather than rely on clinical and hospital referrals because the process by which clients are finally referred to or refer themselves to clinics and hospitals is fraught with structural, linguistic, and cultural problems.

Multilingualism and Aging: The Use of the Verbal Fluency Paradigm

As mentioned in the previous chapter, there is a relatively large amount of literature which has evolved over the years on bilingualism, on the one hand, and aging studies on the other hand, but there is very little research on healthy aging bilinguals (Clyne, 1977; Obler *et al.*, 1980; Rosselli *et al.*, 1999; Rosselli *et al.*, 2000). Obler *et al.* focused on healthy aging subjects. Their study investigated the effects of bilingualism on category fluency (animal list generation) and verbal (phonemic) fluency in which the subjects were asked to generate words that begin with the letters, F, A and S respectively. In the Obler *et al.* study the performance of the bilinguals was reported to be superior to that of monolinguals. The Rosselli *et al.* study compared the performance of Spanish-English bilinguals with that of Spanish and English monolinguals. Their results show that the Spanish-English bilinguals were comparable (not superior) to that of English and Spanish monolinguals in category fluency tasks and the per-formance of the Spanish-English was, however, not influenced by the language used in the assessment. So there is a discrepancy between the Obler *et al.* and Rosselli *et al.* findings on the effects of bilingualism using the verbal fluency task. Obler *et al.* report superior performance for bilinguals, while Rosselli *et al.* suggest that bilingual subjects did not perform better than monolingual subjects. It is difficult to reconcile the dis-crepancy between the two studies because it is possible that there were substantial and qualitative differences in the nature and type of bilingual-ism in the Obler *et al.* and Rosselli *et al.* studies. Unfortunately reconciling the discrepancy between the studies is difficulty because Obler *et al.* do not provide detailed descriptions of their subjects. The impact of bilingualism also varied depending on the tasks used. Bilingualism did not have an effect on verbal (phonemic) fluency but did have on category fluency.

Although the Obler *et al.* and Rosselli *et al.* studies report different bilingual effects on language performance in aging, the studies used a similar research design. Both used a three group design, comparing two monolingual groups: English, and Spanish and Spanish-English bilinguals as in the Rosselli *et al.* study. Roberts and Le Dorze (1998) used what we may call a one group two language design. They compared the perfor-mance of French-English bilinguals in each of their two languages. Their results show that there was no difference in category fluency between the two languages when the results were aggregated. There were differences in the performance of the subjects in the category fluency task, particularly in the animal recall task. The results suggest that the effects of bilingualism in aging may be comparable across languages in some tasks but be different in other tasks across languages. A systematic comparison of the effects of category fluency in the different studies with monolingual studies is rendered difficult because the studies used a wide range of cate-gories in the category fluency tasks. For example, some studies used 'fruits' and 'vegetables' in addition to 'animals' (Bayles & Kaznik, 1987; Kemper *et al.*, 1998), while others, used 'foods' and 'clothing' (Benton *et al.*, 1994). There are some categories which are used less frequently such as 'vehicles', 'things' in a supermarket, 'first names', 'occupations' and 'furniture' (Benton and Hamsher, 1989). In our study we opted to use 'vehicles' although infrequently used as a category because our research site, Detroit, was near an important manufacturing company, General Motors.

The design of the study into African-American bilingualism reported on in this chapter is comparable to the work by Roberts and Le Dorze (1998) in that we compare the performance in each subject between two languages, African-American Vernacular (AAV) and Standard American English (SAE) using two types of tasks frequently used in clinical settings: category and verbal fluency.

Research Questions

In the study reported in this chapter we aimed at evaluating language skills and cognitive functioning in older African-Americans by focusing on lexical aspects of language: verbal and category fluency. We focused on category and verbal fluency because these items have been studied in aging research hence providing opportunities for comparison (Ardilla *et al.*, 1994; Ardilla *et al.*, 2000; Roselli *et al.*, 2000). The following are the specific questions we sought to address:

(1) What are the effects of age on verbal and category fluency?
(2) What are the effects of education on verbal and category fluency? Does the medium through which the tasks are administered, i.e. AAV or SAE, affect the measures on working memory?
(3) Does the medium through which the tasks are administered affect performance on verbal and category fluency?
(4) What are the effects of working memory on verbal and category fluency?

Set up of the Study

In order to address the four research questions above, we selected a number of instruments which were designed to assess: (1) working memory; (2) physical status; (3) verbal and category fluency. It was necessary to assess working memory because it is susceptible to dementia and other cognitive impairments. The second set of instruments was used to assess the physical status of the subjects. The third set of instruments was used to assess verbal and category fluency. In the analysis we compare the effects of age, education, and working memory on verbal and category fluency when assessed in SAE and AAV to investigate whether the medium through which the assessment is carried out affects the results.

The selection of research subjects for any research project is an important aspect of any research project, but it is even more important in aging research. In most psycholinguistic research subjects are selected on the assumption that every member has the potential of being included in the sample. Such an assumption, although valid in most research projects, is of doubtful validity in aging research, because of the difficulties (if not impossibility) of controlling for population mortality (see Chapter 8 on language and epidemiology in the North Manhattan Aging Project). In the African-American community aging project we therefore were not interested in estimating population parameters, but how aging and cognitive impairment might be expressed through bilingual abilities of the research subjects at different degrees of severity 'under conditions which may be idealized or extreme' (Schaie, 1977). Eligible subjects were included in the cognitively intact group in the absence of reported histories of psychiatric illnesses such as brain injury, cerebrovascular disease, epilepsy, depression and substance abuse, and were not impaired on Activities of Daily Living (ADL) cross-validated with performance on the MMSE. Subjects with scores between 10 and 23 on the MMSE and with nine or more years of education were categorized as impaired and the results are not included in this chapter. The MMSE was used for screening purposes and not for diagnostic reasons because of the problematic nature of the MMSE which we alluded to earlier in the chapter. In this chapter we focus on research participants who were categorized as cognitively intact. For all the research subjects, evaluation included short measures of visual and hearing acuity. In order to test hearing acuity, researchers whispered a short phrase and asked the subjects to repeat it.

Research Sites

Research subjects were recruited from the western side of Detroit. It was important to recruit subjects from a very specific geographical and socio-economic area in Detroit (Michigan) because AAV varies geographically, and is influenced by a number of factors notably social class (Smitherman, 2000). According to the 2000 Census, Detroit has a population of 95,270 over the age of 65, 81% of whom are categorized as African-Americans with the remaining 15% made up of whites, Asian, native Hawaiian and Africans. Detroit is the eighth largest city in terms of the number of older Blacks aged 65 and over. Research subjects were recruited from the Tennessee Baptist Church, Beauty Shops, Barber Shops and Detroit Senior Citizens Centers. The church was used as a key recruitment site and point of entry into the local African-American community because churches play a key role in African-American community life, and community based research has to take that into account. The church provided community support for African-Americans and acted as a site for social networking and informal advice, at times providing on the sport medical testing for high blood pressure and other common minor ailments which were felt to affect church members. The recruitment was based on a series of church announcements by a local church priest frequented by Geneva Smitherman who acted as a social consultant for the project particularly for aspects relating to AAV for which she has extensive knowledge and expertise. Membership of the church was a crucial part of the research design in the recruitment strategy. The effectiveness of the recruitment strategy was evident when it came to the recruitment of the 'oldest-old' – 85 years and above. The low signing for the research by the 'oldest-old' might be attributed to their failure to comprehend some of the church announcements particularly as they related to the research project. In seeking to clarify the research one of the 'oldest-old' aptly expressed the issue eloquently when she said she was not going to register for the project because she thought she was expected to pay $25 in order to participate. The intention of the church announcements was contrary to the way she had interpreted the announcement. In the announcement it was said that research subjects would receive $25 for taking part. But the 'oldest-old' woman had construed the announcements contrary to our intentions, giving rise to mis-communication. The mis-communication was resolved, and the differences with the 'oldest-old' woman ironed out, she agreed to take part because as she memorably put it 'she was going to be paid for not remembering'.

The other recruitment site which was of central importance in the project was a hair dressing salon known as the 'Beauty Box' owned by 'M' since the 1970s. The hair dressing salon was situated adjacent to a funeral home, a location appropriate to the hair dressing specialist whose responsibilities included preparing deceased persons' 'hair styles' as well. The hair dressing salon was patronized by women of all generations to have their done and nails polished. The clients were drawn from different professions, legitimate and not so orthodox: 'from boosters to lawyers, from the gutter to the heavens' as 'M' the owner of the Beauty Shop aptly put it. The hair dressing salon was an effective recruitment site because the owner was well known within the Detroit community. 'M' had received recognition for her involvement in serving the needs of her local community. Because of her extensive network and wide client base she was able to get us into contact with prospective research subjects. Because, most African-American women retain the same hair dressing salon for a long period of time we were able to follow up some of the research subjects for further assessment when they reported to the hair dressing salon. In order to dispel any suspicions the local community might have about the research the hair dressing specialist was one of the research subjects to be assessed.

A Description of the Research Participants

The key variables in the description of the demographics of the research subjects were age, gender, marital status, education and medium of assessment. For medium of assessment we were referring to whether the assessment was carried out in either SAE or AAV or both. Table 7.1 presents the demographic characteristics of the research subjects. The age of the research subjects ranged from 46 to 97 with a mean age of 73.7 and a standard deviation (SD) of 11.0. Age was later categorized into 64 or younger, 65 to 74, 75 to 84, and 85 and beyond. The highest frequency of subjects (42%) was within the 65–74 group. There were more females (73%) than males in the sample population. The majority (57%) was widowed and while 80% reported at least eight years of education, half of the sample reported 12 years of education. Demographic information was acquired directly from the research subjects: in the event that the subject could not supply the information, it was obtained by proxy, in most cases from a primary care giver, who might be a sibling or a spouse.

Table 7.1 Characteristics of participants

Age	Number	%	Years of education
64 years or younger	10	19.2	12
65–74	22	42.3	10
75–78	11	21.2	8
85	9	17.3	7
Gender			
Male	12	22.6.	10
Female	41	77.4	8

Education	Number	%
4–7	8	15.1
8–11	21	39.6
12+	24	45.3
Language of Assessment		
Standard American English	21	40.4
African-American Vernacular	31	59.6

The assessment protocol was made up of a combination of health, cognitive and language measures and assessed through AAV and SAE to the same respondent. The health measures were based on the ADL instrument (Katz *et al.*, 1963). The language measures were composed of linguistic items from the Bilingual Aphasia Test (BAT) by Paradis (1987). BAT is an elaborate instrument used to assess a wide range of linguistic skills. The Paradis test, although designed for use with aphasia, is composed of items drawn from previous research studies on dementia. In this study we used the BAT protocol to assess working memory, age, and cognitive status on language (see also Juncos-Rabadán and Iglesias, 1994 of the use of the BAT with aging participants). In aphasia research, the instrument has been validated for use in a lot of languages including Dutch, Spanish, and German. In this chapter we focus on how cognitive, mental health, attention and working memory affect language. The construct of working memory which was used was based on Baddeley (1990), one of the most empirically well supported models of working memory.

Working Memory

The Digit Span test (forward and backward) was used to assess attention and working memory. In Digit Span each research subject was asked to remember strings of numbers ranging from 3 to 9 in the order in which they were given. A maximum possible score was 14. In Digit Span backward the research subject was instructed to remember the numbers in a reverse order. The instructions were given in SAE and AAV respectively. In order to control for the effects of practice the subjects were randomly assigned to two groups, these who were assessed in AAV first and subsequently in SAE and conversely. The AAV and SAE tests were administered in consecutive sessions with an interlude of a week between the two assessments. The following were the instructions in SAE and AAV for Digit Span forward and backward. Digit Span forward instructions in SAE and AAV:

For SAE:
I am going to read you some sets of numbers. Listen carefully, and when I am finished with each set of numbers say them to me in the same order that I read them to you.

For AAV:
I'm gonna read you some sets of numbers. Listen carefully, and when I finish with each set of numbers say them to me in the same order that I read them to you.

For Digit Span backwards, the following instructions were used:

For SAE:

I am gonna to read you some sets of numbers and this time when I am finished with each set of numbers, say them to me backwards. For example, if I say 719 what would you say?

For AAV:

Another measurement of working memory used was Alpha Span. In Alpha Span the research subject was asked to remember strings of words and repeat them in alphabetical order. Because of the relatively low levels of formal literacy, the rhetorical framework for asking the question was changed from repeating them in alphabetical order to repeating them in 'ABC'.

Health Status Measures

Health status and the ability to live and function independently was assessed using two tests on Activities of Daily Living: ADLs and IADLs. ADLs are generally fully acquired between the ages of seven and eight in normal circumstances. IADL (Lawton & Brody, 1969) are more sophisticated and complex than ADLs. Tasks which fall under the rubric of IADL are 'shopping, preparing meals and other types of house chores'.

Mental Health Measures

The MMSE (Folstein *et al.*, 1975) was used as a measure of cognitive impairment, since it has been shown to be sensitive to impairment when the scores are adjusted for education in African-Americans (Lichtenberg, 1998). The MMSE is a 30 item screening instrument. More errors were permitted for the less educated than for the more highly educated African-Americans. African-Americans were allowed one additional error above their white counterparts before they were classified as impaired. Because this is a community-based study and not a clinical study, the MMSE was used to identify older persons who were able to participate but not as a screening instrument for impairment. Because of ethical sensitivity, research subjects who presented cognitive signs of impairment and had no formal diagnosis were strongly urged to refer to the local memory clinic for a full assessment, by professional neuropsychologists.

Verbal and Category Fluency

As indicated before, there were two types of fluency measures: verbal fluency and category fluency. Both were first developed by Guilford (1967) and with some adaptations have been used in aphasia and more recently in dementia studies. The research subjects were individually instructed to recall as many words as possible beginning with the sound, or letter K, P, T, and H. These four letters were chosen because they represented sets of words varying in size; this is reflected by the number of pages for these letters in various dictionaries. For example, the 1991 edition of the Macquarie Dictionary has 18 pages for K, 76 for H, 111 for T and 161 for P. A similar pattern in which there is disparity in the number of words beginning with the stimuli words can also be found in the Oxford Advanced Learners Dictionary: 9 for K, 40 for H, 56 for T and 89 for P. Time was measured using a stopwatch in both verbal and category fluency. Instructions were administered in SAE and AAV.

Category fluency

In category fluency, research subjects were asked to give as many items as possible that were exemplars of *vegetables*, *furniture*, and *cars*. The research subjects were given one minute each, and time was measured using a stopwatch. Items were counted only once. For example, subject CW was awarded a score of four under the category of furniture when she produced the following exemplars of furniture: lamp, table, couch, chair, chair. Respondents were not given any credit for repetition, even if the repetition was only partial. For example, RB produced partial versions of the same item, table, coffee table. The words were written in the actual order in which they were produced by the subject. The raw scores were made up of the total number of admissible words produced by each subject in SAE and AAV versions of the test, irrespective of category.

Results

The mean distributions and standard deviations of measures of working memory and verbal and category fluency, semantic categories, stratified by age, education level, gender and language used for assessment were examined. A series of univariate linear regression analyses were then conducted to explore the relative contribution of age, education, gender and medium of assessment on Digit Span Forward and Digit Span Backward, Alpha Span, MMSE, verbal fluency, category fluency using ages 65–74, grades 4–7, and SAE as reference groups.

Table 7.2 shows the relations between working memory performance and age. For all age groups, the results illustrate that all research subjects did better on Digit span Forward (DSF), and worst on Alpha span (AS), and that the 65–74 age group performed better than the 64 or younger age group. Performance on DSF, DSB and AS declines after the age of 84. Table 7.3 provides information on the relation between age, education, gender and mother tongue on performance on the verbal fluency task. In terms of education, the group with 12 and more years of education had

Table 7.2 Age and working memory measures: Digit span forward: Digit span back: Alpha span

Age	N	M	SD	M	SD	N	M	SD
64–	10	6.60	3.27	5.40	3.44	8	3.13	1.64
65–74	22	8.09	2.67	6.23	2.86	22	5.14	2.08
76–84	10	5.80	2.20	4.60	2.72	9	3.22	1.79
85+	9	6.44	3.43	4.67	1.94	8	2.50	2.39

Table 7.3 Verbal fluency, age, education, gender and mother tongue

Age	N	Mean number of words	SD
64 or younger	8	24.00	9.68
65–74	20	22.70	11.77
75–84	10	13.40	7.62
85+	8	15.38	4.69
Education	N	M	SD
4–7	7	13.57	7.70
8–11	18	17.33	4.83
12+	21	23.62	13.04
Gender			
Female	35	20.26	11.58
Male	11	17.64	4.70
Language			
African-American Vernacular	19	25.11	13.03
Standard American English	26	15.31	5.13

the highest scores relative to other educational groups. There were gender differences but these were not consistent across the different measures. For example, men did better on DSF, and DSB, while women did better on AS than men.

When the results from the different subtests were aggregated best performance was displayed by female research subjects, 65–74, reporting 12 + years of education, when assessed in SAE. Table 7.4 presents the data for category fluency.

In terms of age, the youngest group, 64 or younger, had the highest category fluency scores. The category scores decline with an advance in

Table 7.4 The effect of age, education, gender and language of assessment on category fluency

Age	N	Mean	SD
64 or younger	8	33.88	20.13
65–74	18	31.44	10.97
75–84	10	21.80	8.82
85+	8	23.63	8.65
Education			
4–7	7	23.43	13.62
8–11	18	27.00	8.31
12+	19	31.26	15.78
Gender			
Female	34	28.09	13.52
Male	10	28.90	11.03
Language used in assessment			
Standard American English	19	30.74	16.78
African-American Vernacular	25	26.48	8.80

age, with a substantial drop between 75 and 84, with a slight increase after 85. Although there is a gradual decline with advancement in age, the category scores gradually increase after 85 but only slightly: an incomplete 'U' shaped curve. The group with 12 or more years of education had higher scores than those with less education. There was no difference in terms of performance according to gender. In both verbal and category fluency, the research subjects performed better when assessed in SAE as opposed to AAV. The distribution of mean scores for individual category scores were highest for the age group, 65–74, and declines with an advancement in age. The performance on individual items improves with more years of reported education. Some of the items were sensitive to gender; females had higher scores on vegetables and food items compared to males, who had higher scores for categories such as furniture and cars. Generally, the subjects performed better on category fluency in SAE than in AAV.

Relationships Between Cognitive Measures and Total Category Fluency

First analyses show that the relationships between measures of cognitive status were statistically significant between MMSE and category

Table 7.5 Relationships between working memory measures and fluency measures

	VF	P	CF	P
DSF	r = 0.471	0.001***	r = 0.612	0.001***
DSB	r = 0.385	0.011***	r = 0.670	0.001***
AS	r = 0.461	0.003**	r = 0.741	0.001**

fluency ($r = 0.67$, $p < 0.01$), and but only marginally between MMSE and verbal fluency ($r = 0.44$, $p = 0.072$.)

In Table 7.5 we examine the relationship between measures of working memory and verbal and category fluency.

The results of Table 7.5 show that the relationships between working memory and verbal and category fluency were all statistically significant. Correlations were somewhat higher for category fluency than for verbal fluency.

Discussion and Conclusions

In this chapter we have tried answer our research questions:

(1) Does language performance decline with age in African-American?
(2) Does bilingualism affect language performance?

Language was defined narrowly and strictly to refer to verbal and category fluency. The results demonstrate that optimum performance for the African-Americans was achieved by the 65–74 age group. This is significant because the 65–74 age group performed better than the younger group, but age begins to have an impact after 75 when language declines with age. The fact that language performance does not necessarily decline with age is consistent with research findings from other studies, illustrating the complicated nature of the relationship between language and aging. Using the 65–74 age group as a reference point, the results from the DSF and DSB showed the difference in working memory between 65 and 74 and 85+ was statistically significant.

The research participants were assessed in both their languages separately, AAV and SAE. Contrary to our expectations, the subjects did better on verbal fluency when assessed in SAE than in AAV. From a Dynamic Systems Perspective we are arguing that aging persons do not necessarily benefit when they are assessed in their first language unless they have developed the necessary resources to carry out those tasks in that language; so it is not language *per se* irrespective of whether it is a first or a second, etc.which necessarily results in aging persons being able to perform better; it's whether they have developed the necessary resources to carry out those tasks in that language. In addition, attitudinal resources may come into play. In terms of verbal fluency, we are arguing that aging African-Americans might not necessarily have developed the necessary resources to carry out tasks such as verbal fluency in AAV. The resources to carry out the tasks in AAV were more likely to be directly linked with SAE than AAV. The situation is much more complicated for category fluency. The results of the study show that subjects with 4–7 years of education did better when assessed in SAE than in AAV, while subjects with 8–11 years of education perform better in AAV than in SAE category fluency. The performance of subjects with 12 or more years of education is not affected by the medium through which the assessment is carried out. AAV might not necessarily have a positive effect on verbal fluency because the tasks might in actual fact be indirect measures of literacy, a type of literacy which one might acquire as the subjects got educated. The results might also be construed to mean that for older subjects to being assessed in AAV, a specific level of formal education is necessary. Other results reveal a much more complicated role of bilingualism on category fluency than the Roberts and Dorze study in which the performance across languages was similar in the two languages of the subjects. Another important finding from the study is that bilingualism seems to have a differential effect depending on whether we are referring to verbal or category fluency. The differences between the two tasks are consistent with findings in the Rosselli _et al._ (2000) study. One explanation might be that category fluency tasks seek to elicit concrete nouns, whereas verbal fluency does not. Concrete nouns may share comparable features across the two languages of the bilinguals in their representations, unlike non-concrete nouns which are elicited in verbal fluency. Another difference between the tasks may arise from the fact that category fluency correlates with lexical knowledge while verbal fluency correlates with executive function tasks.

The data show a complex picture in which only the role of education is clear: higher levels of education go with higher fluency scores. This is in line with many other studies on the role of education in age-related changes in behavior.

Many questions remain unanswered: Are the findings representative of other groups of African-Americans? How do findings on fluency tasks relate to other measures of language proficiency and to what extent is working memory rather than age the defining variable in the differences between age groups? Obviously, larger-scale multi-site projects are needed to assess the relation between language and aging in different minority groups before we can reach any generalizable conclusion.

The chapter is part of a broader project which sought to analyze the effects of bilingualism on the neurocognitive and linguistic performance of older African-Americans. Bilingualism in this chapter is construed to refer to the ability to use AAV and SAE. The study was faced with both practical and conceptual problems. Practically, the study was confronted with the problems of recruiting and retaining older African-Americans given that older African-Americans are generally skeptical of taking part in most research. The church and hair dressing salons proved to be important recruitment sites. Conceptually, the study sought to design tasks which are of equal degree of difficulty between AAV and SAE. The study makes an important contribution not only to issues about language in health in older African-Americans, but deepens our understanding of the social and clinical contexts within which bilingual older African-Americans use language, and the role of bilingualism in an assessment of cognition because until recently, research into AAV was largely historical and structural. The results demonstrate the complexities of bilingualism on neurocognitive assessment, and language performance. The results suggest that,at least for older African-Americans, they do not necessarily always perform better when assessed in AAV. Superior performance in AAV is dependent upon education, and the nature of the task being administered, and the individual's experience and from a Dynamic Systems Theory perspective the resources which the informant can exploit when being assessed. In some cases, the informant might be able to draw upon more resources from a second language than from a first language, hence perform 'better' in a second language than in a first language. In order to get a comprehensive picture of the informants' cognitive capacity it might be necessary to assess some tasks in one language, and others are in a different language. The question which is the best language of assessment for all the tasks is misleading. The question should be which language should be used to get a more comprehensive picture of cognitive status at a specific point in time. The effects of bilingualism in aging may be much more complicated than we initially thought. The effects may also not only depend upon the nature of the task, and other linguistic factors but with the nature and type of bilingualism itself, and the ways in which the bilingualism interacts with the medication which the informants are taking given the fact that most elderly persons are on a wide range of drugs. The nature of the medication an elderly informant is on may interact in complex ways which have an impact on language performance in ways which are currently not systematically documented. The study focused on older African-Americans drawing the informants from a strictly bounded geographical area in Detroit. The advantage of drawing upon informants from a strictly bounded geographical area is that we were able to control for factors such as migration history, socio-economic status, etc. The disadvantage is that the results may not necessarily be applicable to other African-American communities which have a different migration history and socio-economic status than those in the Detroit study.

Chapter 8

The Effects of Age and Education on Narrative Complexity in Older Chinese in the USA

SINFREE MAKONI with HWEI-BIN LIN and ROBERT SCHAUF

This chapter reports on a study which examined the effects of age, and education on grammatical and narrative skills in elderly Chinese, particularly storytelling. While we did not conceptualize the research reported here within the Dynamic Systems Theory perspective (see Chapter 10), some remarks on how DST would illuminate the data will help situate the work reported here with the wider aims of this book.

From a cognitive perspective, storytelling may by variously modeled. For simplicity's sake, two current (dominant) paradigms are: Information Processing Theory and Dynamic Systems. In both cases, the act of telling a story involves (minimally) the integration of various mental representations, ranging from sensory imagery (visual, auditory, haptic, etc.), emotion, language (either as reported speech or as an internal medium of information processing; Carruthers, 2002; Schrauf, 2002), and narrative coherence. (Much the same integration of kinds of information occurs in autobiographical memory; Rubin, 1998). From an information processing perspective, however, these mental representations are understood to come together – some serially, some in parallel – as the story comes on-line and is 'translated' or performed in speech.

The Dynamic Systems view places rather more emphasis on parallel (vs. serial) processing and a constantly occuring feedback loops. For DST, it is less useful to think in terms of 'mental representations' coming together like so many building blocks, and more useful to think of an emerging picture coming into focus as massive amounts and varied kinds of 'information' flows into consciousness. Importantly, schematic forms guide the integration of information but not as templates-to-be-filled in but rather as emerging forms themselves. Rarely is a story told twice in exactly the same way: contexts change, purposes change, interlocutors change, the story-teller him / herself changes.

Our argument here is that older individuals preserve their storytelling abilities despite various (age-related but not pathological) cognitive decrements and that these abilities are not correlated with education (hence the utility of narrative complexity as a cognitive screen). Either theory (DST or information processing) is amenable to our empirical work, but we suspect that DST may present a 'truer' picture of how the aging brain can recruit new resources and strategies in the performance of complex cognitive activities – storytelling among them. We also suspect that as age-related changes in cognition occur across the brain, a much touted 'graceful degradation' – due in part to massive parallel circuitry – preserves storytelling almost completely. Except where the reavages approach dementia.

We elicited stories aimed at investigating the narrative and syntactic complexity in the storytelling of cognitively intact Chinese elderly using visual stimuli to control for the effects of literacy on task performance. The study is part of a larger project whose ultimate aim is to examine the role of age, and education and the potential significance of storytelling as a diagnostic instrument in the assessment of persons who are functionally impaired with or without dementia. Although the study focused on functional impairment, it was anticipated that a screen for functional impairment will be able to capture most dementias. Many of the neuropsychological instruments used in the assessment of dementia are biased with respect to education (Neill, 2001), the language of administration and the nature of the interaction between the researcher and the subjects, and the interpretation of a specific score is confounded by educational and cultural factors. In an attempt to circumvent the educational and cultural factors we sought to test storytelling as a pancultural cognitive task common for both educated and non-educated elderly individuals. The chapter is divided into two main sections. The first section reviews the literature on Chinese aging, the second part outlines how the data which forms the basis of this chapter was collected and analyzed.

Language and Aging in the Chinese Community

In order to contextualize this study of narrative production among Chinese elders, literature relevant to aging in this particular group is discussed here. The first strand comments on the research on Chinese aging distinguishing between two types of research on Chinese aging in East Asia as opposed to Chinese aging as immigrants in the USA: a distinction aptly referred to by Jackson (2002) as 'aging in place of origin' as opposed to 'aging out of place of origin'. The second strand focuses on narrative development in children, pathological adults, and elderly persons.

In this section we focus on research on Chinese aging which falls under the rubric of what Jackson (2002: 829) refers to as 'descriptive comparative research'. In 'descriptive comparative research' the analyst focuses on describing similarities and differences between groups either within the same country or across national boundaries. An illustration of a 'descriptive comparative research' is the research comparing the well-being of rural and urban Chinese 'oldest-old' in China (Yi & Vaupel, 2002). A second example of 'descriptive comparative research' is a comparison of Chinese intergenerational relations in Australia and the United States (Noels *et al.*, 1999). The study by Yi and Vaupel (2002) on the functional capacity and self-evaluation of the health and life of the 'oldest old' in China is useful and illuminating because although China is the most populous country in the world our knowledge of the nature of aging, particularly in the 'oldest-old' in China, is regrettably extremely limited (Antonucci *et al.*, 2002). In a way consistent with a 'descriptive comparative research' Yi and Vaupel (2002) analyse the functional cognitive and physical capabilities of the 'oldest old' in two contexts: rural and urban China. Based on a longitudinal study which includes a total of 8805 people, 2000 of whom, interestingly enough, were centenarians, their results suggest that the rural elderly were in better cognitive and physical status than their urban counterparts for a number of reasons, one of the most salient being that there are more opportunities for physically exerting work in rural than in urban China. A healthy diet and less environmental pollution in rural areas are among the contributing factors. In spite of the differences between rural and urban Chinese elderly, the study also reported gender differences in the 'oldest old' Chinese. The 'oldest old' women were more susceptible to cognitive and physical decline than their male counterparts.

From a linguistic perspective another interesting aspect of the Yi and Vaupel study is the way the researchers adapted the internationally and extensively used Mini Mental Status Examination (MMSE) (Folstein *et al.*, 1975) to suit the socio-educational conditions of the 'oldest-old' in China. In the Chinese version of the MMSE a number of questions were revised. For example, in the orientation section of the MMSE the question 'what is the year?' was changed to ' What is the animal year of this year'? The change to 'animal year' was necessary because not all the 'oldest old' Chinese are familiar with the Western calendar. Instead of asking the subjects to read and write a sentence, which presupposed a level of literacy, the question was replaced by asking the informants to name as many *foods* as possible, a question which proved meaningful even to the Chinese 'oldest-old' and consequently could be expected to have high ecological validity. The question on calculation was also simplified because a majority of Chinese elderly have no formal education and are therefore likely not to be numerate. This adaptation of the MMSE to the Chinese 'oldest old' is revealing given our earlier critique of the linguistic aspects of the MMSE in the chapter on language in older African-Americans.

Communication Accommodation Theory and Chinese Aging

Most of the research which has been carried out on intergenerational relations among communities of Chinese elders has been conducted under the intellectual framework of Communication Accommodation Theory (CAT) associated with the work of Giles *et al.* (1992), Fox and Giles (1993), and the related framework of the Communication Predicament Model (CPM) (Ryan *et al.*, 1986; Ryan & Norris, 2001). In this chapter we only briefly describe some of the key features of the models. It is important, however, to bear in mind that CAT and CPM were neither originally conceptualized as explanatory frameworks for aging nor are they restricted to it, so their use in aging can be construed as a type of applied exercise. CAT is founded on the principle that when 'individuals encounter others from another social group, they tend to treat them as members of that social category, rather than as individuals' (Noels *et al.*, 2001: 250). Because of the negative stereotypes younger adults have of older persons they may tend to 'overaccommodate'. This 'overaccommodation' is characterized by the use of 'elderspeak' with linguistic features such as excessive repetition and a generally slow rate of delivery. The use of 'elderspeak' may have negative consequences on the speech capabilities of elderly persons which are captured by the CPM (Harwood & Giles, 1996, Bartolucci & Henwood, 1986). The use of 'elderspeak' subtly excludes older persons from conversational engagement that could help them to sustain and indeed develop their abilities. Their non-participation confirms the perceptions by the younger generation that aging is a period of decline and reaffirms (perhaps unconsciously) their use of excessively simplified talk. This may lead to a downward spiral in which the elderly person appropriates and acts out the image of being incompetent and is met by the younger adult's continued use of more simplified talk, so there are two kinds of negative spirals: one which has to do with negative image and the reaction of younger generations on it and the depreciating that follows, and one which is mechanical and has to do with use as exercise. Nominally, the intergenerational relations of Chinese elderly are characterized by a strong sense of filial piety and pressure to obey their elderly persons *'xiao shuen'* (Noels *et al.* 1999).

Because of the strong pressure and need to obey it is logical to expect that there will be a strong sense of deference towards the elderly, more so in Chinese communities than in Western countries. Contrary to our expectations, the research among older individuals from East Asian countries and the Chinese communities in Hong Kong suggest that there was less deference to elderly persons in the Chinese communities than in Western countries such as the United States and Australia in spite of the strong nominal commitment to filial piety in the Chinese. This may be explained as the outcome of what Noels *et al.* refer to as 'evaluative backlash' against older persons in Chinese communities. It is, however, not clear from the research cited whether the erosion of intergenerational relations occurs in both public and private situations. In some non-Western communities, intra-family generational relations do not necessarily follow the same pattern as intergenerational relations in the public space (Makoni, 1997). In the Chinese situation, if intra-familial generational relations do not necessarily follow the same pattern as relations in the public space, then the erosion of expressions of filial piety may not be easily extended to intra-familial relations as well.

Comparative Research on Aging

While the research on Chinese aging carried out within the framework of the CAT and CPM has focused largely on the impact of intergenerational relations on subjective health and functional well-being, another strand of research on Chinese aging has focused more narrowly on the significance of acculturation on physical and functional impairment. This type of research is referred to by Jackson (2002: 803) as 'comparative research processes', a type of research which seeks to 'understand what processes of aging may be influenced by factors such as national origin, culture, acculturative factors, and race/ethnicity. For us in Chinese aging a 'comparative research process' involves two types of research. Firstly, studies comparing the Chinese 'aging in place' with those 'aging out of place', requires comparing Chinese aging in mainland China, Hong Kong and Taiwan compared with those aging in the United States. Unfortunately, we could not readily find examples of studies comparing the Chinese 'aging in place' and 'aging out of place'. The second strand of a 'comparative research process' involves comparing the Chinese 'aging out of place' with other immigrant groups also 'aging out of place'. An excellent example of the latter is the study comparing the effects of 'acculturation' between Chinese and the Vietnamese elderly immigrants in

California (Morton *et al.*, 1992). Acculturation has been reported to have important health and social outcomes for ethnic minorities. The effects of 'acculturation' have been observed to include a wide range of behaviors notably socio-political issues such as conflict resolution (Kagan *et al.*, 1977) personality characteristics (Sue & Kirk, 1972) and utilization of health services and sustainance of treatment regimen (Miranda, 1976). Research on 'acculturation' in Chinese aging has two main strands. The first strand focuses on the construct of 'acculturation', the second focuses on the role of language proficiency, particularly English language proficiency among Chinese in the United States and its contribution to 'acculturation'. The Suinn-Lew Asian Self Identity Acculturation Scale (SL-ASIA has been critiqued by Morton *et al.*). Morton *et al.* (1992) argue that although the SL-ASIA 'acculturation' scale was originally derived from research with Asian Americans it was flawed for four main reasons. Firstly, it was construed as lacking important dimensions. It lacked a structural assimila-tion component, which is unfortunate because 'structural assimilation' may occur with or without 'acculturation'. Secondly, the SL-ASIA was validated for only a small sample of university students. Thirdly, although the SL-ASIA scale has a language dimension it does not distinguish between different Asian communities, some of the most visible being Koreans, Japanese and Chinese, etc. Fourthly, the scale is not sufficiently sensitive to the situationally embedded nature of human behavior, so it does not satisfactorily take cognizance of the contextually bound nature of ethnic behavior. Morton *et al.* (1992) take the research into 'acculturation' in Chinese one step further. They compare the effects of 'acculturation' on the functional impairment of older Chinese and Vietnamese communities residing in California and they investigate the role of the English language proficiency in the 'acculturation' processes. The study demonstrated that low English language proficiency was positively correlated with func-tional impairment in the older Chinese community, but not in the Vietnamese community where low English language proficiency was not significantly correlated with either functional impairment nor with the capacity to make use of health resources. Morton *et al.* suggest that low English language proficiency did not affect functional impairment in the Vietnamese community in California because the Vietnamese community in California is much more cohesive while the Chinese community in Cali-fornia is less intergrated because it is dispersed across California. They speculate that the extensiveness and cohesiveness of the Vietnamese community in California mitigates against the potentially adverse effects of low English language proficiency, while the sparsity of the Chinese community in California exacerbated functional impairment because it meant that the Chinese in California were much more dependent on

English language proficiency to negotiate their social roles than the Vietnamese. It is possible that the role of low English language proficiency in the functional impairment of the Chinese may have exaggerated the role of English because the study was based on 'self report data', and not 'objective' assessment. The study also did not take into account the different varieties of Chinese and the contexts in which these varieties were used. It is possible that too much significance has been placed on 'acculturation' as a contributing factor to physical and mental impairment. There are two key factors which might also have a bearing on the physical and mental impairment other than 'acculturation' which might explain the differences between the Chinese and Vietnamese whose significance has not been examined. Firstly, the dynamics of intra-family relations within the Chinese and Vietnamese communities have not been examined. Secondly, we also don't have information about the time when the Chinese and Vietnamese migrated to the United States. It is also known that the mode of assimilation may vary depending on whether the informants migrated to the United States early or late in life. Migration in late life is increasing and accelerating resulting in more elders leaving their countries of origins late in life to join family members (Portes & Rumbaut, 1996). The exact impact of such late life migration on the acculturation patterns of both groups have not been systematically examined in the study comparing the Chinese and Vietnamese elderly. There might be cohort differences as well depending on when they immigrated to the USA, for example, before or after World War II.

After commenting on the literature on Chinese aging which focuses on intergenerational relations and the construction of acculturation and the role of English language proficiency, we now turn to research on aging which is much more narrowly linguistic. We now concentrate on the research into the narrative and syntactic abilities in children, pathological adults and aging persons. The comments are not restricted to studies which explicitly focus on Chinese because there is very little research on narrative and syntactic complexity in Chinese ageing persons. To the best of our knowledge this chapter pioneers the field on narrative and syntactic complexity in Chinese aging, so the discussion will draw on the extant literature on children, pathological adults and aging persons from other ethnic groups.

Storytelling as a Diagnostic Tool

In this study on elderly Chinese we investigated the potential of storytelling as a diagnostic tool, controlling for the effects of education and age on narrative and syntactic complexity. We focus on storytelling because it is an activity that is highly valued in both literate and non-literate societies (Finnegan, 1970; Heath, 1983; Scholes & Kellog, 1966; Obler & Albert, 1984). All older persons, irrespective of formal education and setting can naturally be expected to have told stories in their lives and may continue to do so even in their advanced age. We expect that storytelling is not as highly biased in favor of the formally educated as other formal linguistic tasks such as word suppliance, grammatical and semantic judgments frequently used in diagnostic assessments. We also felt that stories elicited through visual cues – in our case using a series of line drawings-which did not require any reading or other literacy skills associated with schooling, might facilitate performance among participants with fewer years of formal education. We also sought to investigate storytelling because narratives have been shown to be susceptible to the effects of dementia and aphasia in ethnic minorities such as African-Americans (Ulatowska *et al.*, 2000). At a discourse level disorders of narrative structure and cohesion provide an invaluable window into the occurrence, nature and perhaps character of developmental disorders (Ulatowska *et al.*). In the following section we focus on aspects of narrative development in three populations: children, cognitively intact adults and impaired adults.

Voluminous research has been conducted on the development of children's narrative abilities. The research suggests that children progress in their narrative capacity through progressive stages (Berman & Slobin, 1994). In the early stages children's narratives are largely descriptive, and do not have any readily discernible formal structures. Also in their early stages, when children use cohesive devices, the range of such cohesive devices is extremely limited. This early stage is followed by a more advanced stage in which there is a deployment of a wider range of cohesive devices. At this stage relations between propositions are grammaticalized resulting in a production of narratives which are much more tightly drawn. The development of narrative competence requires necessary cognitive resources, if the narrative events are to be organized in a causal and temporal sequence. The temporal and causal sequence will be organized in a mode consistent with the social scripts and schemas of the communities the children are part of (Rumelhart, 1975; Minsky, 1977; Schank & Abelson, 1977). The capacity to organize events sequentially is buttressed by the ability to deploy attentional and working memory resources for the organization and linkage of different elements of the story. As pointed out in an earlier chapter the model frequently used to explain the nature and function of working memory is the one developed by Baddeley (1986). In the Baddeley model the production and processing of stories involves the use of two slave systems both controlled by the Central Executive System: the phonological and the visuo-spatial systems. A fuller description of the working memory model and how it has been adapted to bilingual contexts is provided in Chapter 4. Defining narrative competence as a function critically dependent on working memory resources is particularly relevant when investigating the storytelling of elderly persons whose working memory capacity may be seen to diminish over time (Craik & Byrd, 1982). This situation is more severe for those suffering from dementia since working memory impairment is one of the hallmarks of dementia particularly Alzheimer's disease.

Gender does seem to result in the production of different narratives between boys and girls (Wodak, 1981, 1986). Wodak suggests that boys and girls produce different types of narratives. Narratives by girls tend to be 'descriptive' while boys' narratives according to Wodak are more 'analytic'. Wodak attributes this difference to differences in socialization. Boys, on the one hand, are socialized into positively valuing analytical thinking while girls, on the other hand, are socialized into being emotionally expressive.

Another area in which narratives have been used is in situations of language pathology. The primary objective of the Ulatowska *et al.* (2000) study was to characterize the salient features of African-American discourse of aphasics and non-aphasics in a battery of discourse tasks. Ulatowska *et al.* focused on African-Americans because a majority of studies have focused on Causasians and very limited research has been focused on African-Americans in spite of their higher degree of susceptibility to neurogenic diseases. This research has focused on repetitions in the narratives of cognitively normal and aphasic African-Americans. Following Tannen (1987), Ulatowska *et al.* identify two types of repetition: the 'self' and 'other' (or allo-repetition as it is technically called). In general the speech of African-Americans is characterized by a high degree of repetition (Smitherman, 1997, 2000). In the chapter on language in aging African-Americans we explored the implications of the different narrative styles of African-Americans on diagnostic assessment which might lead some people being inaccurately classified as incoherent hence probably demented. The misclassification is more likely to occur among people who have been designated 'border–zone dementias' and 'border–zone non-dementias'. 'Border-zone dementias' are defined as elderly people who show incipient or ambiguous signs of dementia. 'Border-zone non-dementias' are those who are not diagnosed as dementias but who show signs of cognitive impairment (Gurland *et al.*, 1997).

Because of the wide prevalence of repetition in African-American speech Ulatowska *et al.* have sought to investigate the extent to which repetition was either maintained or lost due to aphasia in African-Americans. The Ulatowska *et al.* findings demonstrate that repetition is well retained in

African-Americans even among those with aphasia. Subtle differences were, however, noticed between those diagnosed with and those diagnosed without aphasia. The repetition in informants suffering from aphasia was less flexible than the normal subjects. There were also noticeable differences in narrative length between informants with aphasia from those that did not have aphasia. The narratives of those with aphasia were generally shorter than those without aphasia. The narratives of those with aphasia were not only shorter but were less repetitive as well. The relative robustness and continuity of repetition even in those with aphasia might be due to the widespread use of repetition in African-Americans and its social significance in the premorbid health careers of aphasia subjects. Repetition has social significance in the speech of African-Americans because it is used as an expression of social engagement in conversation. In spite of the preserved repetition in aphasia subjects and its social significance, some of the subtle differences might have been missed because of the sampling and analytical procedures used in the Ulatowska *et al.* study in which only mildly impaired aphasics were selected. It therefore remains an open empirical question whether repetition, in spite of its important role in conversation in African-Americans, is retained even among severely impaired aphasics. A more fine tuned analysis focusing on suprasegmental features such as vowel prolongation might have revealed some significant differences.

Narrative Skills in Aging

Studies which have investigated the narrative competence of elderly informants tend to focus on the role of working memory. In the literature on narrative skills in the elderly as discussed in Chapter 2 the general consensus is that such skills are less vulnerable than lexical skills. Here we want to focus on a specific aspect: the role of education. In the discussion on the use of narratives in aging we analyze two main studies, the first by Juncos-Rabádan (1996) and the second by Kemper *et al.* (1990) which are two of the key studies exploring the effects of age, education and language on storytelling capacity in aging. The two studies operationalized narrative complexity in different ways, and as an introduction to the study described below, a review of these is provided. Juncos-Rabádan (1996) asked 184 subjects (94 between the ages of 50 and 60, 90 between 70 and 91 years old) living in Spain (Galicia and Catalonia) and Canada (Montreal and Ottawa), to tell the 'Nest story' from the Bilingual Aphasia Test (BAT) (Paradis, 1987). The story contains six panels depicting a woman directing a man's attention to a bird's nest in a tree, the man climbing the tree to get to the nest, and tree branch breaking and the man falling, the man lying on the ground, the ambulance taking the man away, and the woman visiting the man in hospital. Juncos-Rabadán adopted a Story Grammar approach (Johnson-Laird, 1983) to this story, analyzing its component parts as: setting, location, beginning, plus three subordinate developments, each including four subcomponents (complex reaction + simple reaction + goal; goal-path + attempt to achieve goal + outcome), and finally the ending. Analyzed in this way, the story has 17 structural sense units. Participants are measured on how many of these they report plus how much additional detail they give for each unit beyond the essentials. Other outcome measures include: number of tangential sentences, number of descriptive sentences, number of cohesion links (so, because, then, etc.), and numbers of place deixis used. Each of these outcome measures was regressed on continuous variables of age and years of education. Findings were that individuals in the older age group produced simpler structures, fewer sense-units and fewer cohesion functions than the middle-aged group. Nevertheless, older participants were more descriptive in the stories than younger people. Overall, education correlated with performance. In this study, then, narrative complexity was measured by having individuals describe the action in a series of of cartoon panels and counting the number of units described. The complexity was in the stimulus, and participants either reflected it in their reports or did not.

Another method of testing narrative complexity is to have participants tell a story that they themselves make up. Thus, Kemper *et al.* (1990) asked participants to 'tell us a story – made up like you might tell a child . . . you could then decide to retell a familiar strory or make one from scratch' (p. 208). Kemper *et al.* adopted a scoring system for narrative complexity from earlier work with children by Botvin and Sutton-Smith (1977). These latter authors devised a seven level descriptive system of narrative complexity and used it to show that children acquire the successive levels of complexity from ages 3 to 11. Since the system figures in Kemper *et al.*'s work and in our own work with elderly Chinese, we describe these stages in more detail (These descriptions were loosely inspired by the 'Frog, Where are You?' (Mayer, 1996) story and are not completely the same as those found in the Botvin and Sutton-Smith study.

Level 1. The narrative description is simply a series of events without any causal or temporary connection. 'The boy fell asleep. The frog jumped out of the window'.
Level 2. The narrative contains what Botvin and Sutton-Smith call 'one nuclear dyad'. This is an action and reaction/consequence. 'The frog jumped out of the window.The boy went after him.'
Level 3. A secondary plot element is interposed in the dyad between the

action and the reaction/consequence. 'The frog jumped out of the window.The boy woke up and tripped on the empty jar.The boy went after the frog'.

Level 4. The narratives concatenate two dyadic sequences but eliminate the intervening strictures seen in Level 3. 'The boy fell asleep.The frog jumped out of the window. The boy went after him. The frog saw the dog. The frog ran away.'

Level 5. The narrative contains more than one dyadic sequence and intervening actions within these dyadic sequences. 'The frog jumped out of the window. The boy woke up and tripped on the empty jar. The boy went after the frog. The frog saw a dog. The frog ran up a tree. The dog barked and went away.'

Level 6. At this level, elementary embedding takes place, so that a subplot interrupts the main action and comes to fruition before the main action continues. 'The frog jumped out of the window. The boy woke up and tripped on the jar. He hurt his hand when he fell and his mother ran cold water on it. After his mother put him to bed again, he went out of the window after the frog.'

Level 7. Multiple subplots are embedded in multiple dyadic sequences. (Kemper *et al.* added another level to this schema.)

Level 8. The narrative is followed by an evaluation, what is often called a 'coda'.

Additional aspects included in the study were an analysis of syntactic complexity, a propositional analysis (idea units and the coordinate and subordinate connections between them), and a cohesion analysis. Participants ($N = 62$) were divided into three age groups (60–69, 70–79, 80–90). Regarding narrative complexity, the study showed that the two older groups told more complex stories than the younger group, but this seems to have represented a trade-off because syntactic complexity declined across age groups.

Taken together, these two studies present conflicting findings. The first suggests that narrative complexity decreases with normal aging, the second suggests that it does not. Nevertheless, this may be due to different task demands made in the two studies. In the first, every participant was presented with a story of the same complexity and asked to mirror it in speech production. In the second, participants were asked to make up their own stories. In the latter case, participants control their own production and have greater control over the management of their own cognitve resources. Thus, they may in fact rely more on automated processes (for example pre-stored chunks of speech or story lines) in generating their narratives. This would increase the complexity of the story without overly taxing working memory. On the other hand, the latter situation may well be more telling in a test situation of dementia since the breakdown of these resources would be indicative of greater decrements.

The Study on Chinese Narratives

For these reasons, in the study we report below, with Chinese elders in New York City, we asked participants to simply tell a story based on the Cookie Theft Picture from the Boston Diagnostic Aphasia Exam. A number of actions occur in this one-line drawing and participants can connect these actions narratively, but there is no constraint to do so (as with the Nest story from BAT) and participants may call on whatever linguistic and narrative resources (automatic or controlled) they choose in telling the story: also, since the participant has a picture available throughout his or her narration, in order to lower demands on working memory. We adopted the coding scheme from Kemper *et al.* because it probes for the nested structure of narratives, and this correlates nicely with the dynamics of short-term information storage and manipulation.

The following are the two main specific questions which we sought to address:

(1) To what extent are there age-related differences on narrative and syntactic complexity?
(2) To what extent are there education related differences on narrative and syntactic complexity?

Research site

The research was carried out in the oldest Chinese senior center on the east coast, City Hall Senior Center. The Center sponsored by Hamilton-Madison House was inaugurated on May 24, 1951 in the borough of Manhattan, in New York City. After the tragic events of September 11, 2001, the Center was relocated to the current address: 100 Gold Center, Manhattan, New York which is situated in the vicinity of Chinatown and New York City financial districts. In 2002, it attracted between 300 and 350 members daily. Chinatown has the largest concentration of Chinese in North America but it has increasingly become diverse as it begins to attract other ethnic minorities, notably Puerto Ricans, Burmese, Vietnamese and Filipinos. According to the press release of May 22, 1951, the objective of the Center was to provide an environment in which elderly Chinese 'may spend time talking with friends, drinking tea, playing Chinese checkers, reading Chinese newspapers, listening to Chinese music, watching television, and developing handicraft skills for which the Chinese are famous'. There are two types of elderly Chinese who attend the

Center: one group travels to the Center on its own. The second group is accompanied by either a professional care giver or a family member. The Center also offers ESL lessons and citizenship classes for elderly Chinese immigrants. US immigrants can take a citizenship 'test' in English five years after receiving their 'green cards'.

We made our first visit to the Center in April 2002. During our initial visits we described the objectives of our research to the Center's administrators. The support of the Center administrators was subsequently to prove invaluable during the recruitment of research participants. This chapter focuses only on the data from the elderly subjects who were cognitively intact according to their performance on the Short Portable Mental Status Questionnaire (SPMSQ). After the researchers had fully explained the purpose of the research project in either Cantonese or Mandarin, the subject signed a consent form. The language which was used in the assessment depended on the informant's preference. In some cases the subjects code-switched between languages. The switch was usually from Hakka, and Cantonese to Mandarin rather than vice versa. The assessment lasted between two and a half and three hours per subject. The subjects were not paid for taking part in the project unlike those in the African-American study reported in Chapter 7 on language assessment in African-Americans. Participants were, however, given a small gift (toiletries) as a token of appreciation for taking part in the project. Some subjects refused to take part, attributing their refusal to a lack of formal education. One subject, sadly, but succinctly put it when he said in Cantonese: 'Ngo ji xiuho beje Ngo ge nou m de je kemdo. Ngo ge nou m ho' (I only have elementary education and my brain cannot remember so much and my brain is not good enough).

Participants

The sample comprised 12 individuals which included 5 females and 7 males ranging in age from 63 to 78 (M = 70.25, SD = 5.66). Years of education ranged from 4 to18 (M = 12.83, SD = 4.53). All subjects were born in mainland China except for one subject who was born in New York.

Data collection procedures

All participants were screened for cognitive impairment using the SPMSQ (Pfeiffer, 1975). No impaired subjects were admitted to the sample. Eleven subjects made no errors on the test, one individual made one error. Digit forward and backward were also administered to each participants. Digit forward measures attentional capacities (freedom from distractability), digit backward is a measure of working memory (Lezak, 1995) The latter is of more significance in this study because narrative and syntactic complexity make greater demands on working memory in normal aging (Kemper, 1990). The narratives were elicited by asking the subjects to describe the five Cookie Theft Picture test from the Boston Diagnostic Aphasia Examination. In addition, the narration of a most unforgettable childhood memory was also collected. The questionnaires were issued in one of the classrooms at the Center. To avoid any possible distraction, only the tester and the subject were inside the testing room. All the subjects' responses were recorded onto a SONY audio-cassette tape recorder. Each subject's responses were on an individual audio-cassette tape. During the test, the tester also recorded the responses in ink.

Narratives were coded for complexity using the procedures outlined in Kemper *et al.* (1990). Coding discriminations and examples of narratives corresponding to each level are outlined in Table 8.1.

Results

For the sample as a whole, scores on narrative complexity ranged from 2 to 6 (M = 3.25, SD 1.48). For measures of syntactic complexity analyses were isolated on the basis of natural sentence boundaries plus units comprising pauses coinciding with sentence boundaries followed by repetitions, rephrasings, or revisions. Mean length of utterance (MLU) was calculated by averaging the number of words per utterance. (1) The mean MLU for the sample was 5.90 (SD = 2.66) and ranged from 3.52 to 12. As in Kemper *et al.* (1990) a measure of syntactic fluency was computed by counting numbers of fillers in each narrative; (2) computing percentages of complete sentences among all utterances; and (3) computing percentage of fragments among all utterances.

The results must be read with some caution because some subjects did not provide complete sentences. Therefore, the mean scores on complete versus fragmentary utterances for the sample as a whole is low (complete mean = 39%; SD = 0.27; fragmentary mean = 61%; SD = 0.27).

Correlations among these variables (narrative complexity, MLU, complete utterances, age, years of education, digit forward, and digit backward) are reported in Table 8.2. Only two correlations are significant at the $p < 0.5$ level. Both concern measures of syntactic complexity. As might be expected, the number of years of education correlates significantly with MLU, and digit backward correlates significantly with percentage of complete utterances. Again not surprisingly, this latter suggests that as the resources of working memory decrease, narratives will be marked by more fragmentary utterances. For our purposes the lack of significant correlation between education and narrative complexity may indicate that the ability to narrate simple memories is not confounded by

Table 8.1 Coding for narrative complexity

	Discriminations	*Example*
1.	Simple chaining of events with no temporal or causal connections	有 一 棵樹 有 一個 人 有 You yi ke shu. You yi ge ren. You Have one cl- tree have one cl- person have 一個 公 園． yi ge gueng uan. one cl- park (There is a tree. There is a man. There is a park.)
2.	Chaining of events with some temporal and causal connections noted.	有 一 個 人 在 公 園裡 看到一 You yi ge ren zai gueng uan li kan dao yi Have one cl- person inside park see one cl- 棵 樹上 有一 窩鳥 他想 捉 鳥． ke shu shang you yi wo niao. Ta xiang zhuo niao. tree top have one cl- bird he want catch bird (A man in the park saw a tree. On the tree top, there is a bird nest. He wants to catch the birds.)
3.	Emerging hierarchical structure, with one complex event including a beginning (problem statement), development, and ending (resolution)	有 一個人 很喜 歡 鳥 看 到 樹 上 You yi ge ren hen xi huan niao. Kan dao shu shang Have one cl- person very like bird see tree top 有 一窩鳥 爬上 去 捉 鳥 結 果 跌 you yi wo niao. Pa shang qu zhuo niao. Jie guo dien have one cl- bird climb up catch bird as a result fall 下來 xia lai. Down (There is a man who likes birds very much. He saw a bird nest on the tree top. He climbs up the tree and caught the birds. As a result, he fell down.)
4.	Hierarchical structure with multiple events embedded in each episode	有 一個 男 人 和 一個 女 人 到 You yi ge nan ren han yi ge nu ren dao Have one cl- ma and one cl- come 公 園 散步 公 園 有 一 棵大 樹 gueng uan san bu. Gueng uan you yi ke da shu. park take a walk Park have one cl- big tree 樹 上 有 一 窩 鳥 shu shang you yi wo niao. tree top have one cl- bird 有 一隻 母 鳥和 三隻 小 鳥 You yi zhr mu niao han san zhr xiao niao. Have one cl- mother bird and tree cl- small bird (A man and a woman took a walking in the park. There was a tree in the park. There was a bird nest on the tree top. There were a mother bird and three little birds.)

Table 8.1(*cont.*) Coding for narrative complexity

5.	Hierarchical structure, multiple embedded events that are themselves complex (see No. 3)	有 一 個 男 人 和 一 個 女 人 到 You yi ge nan ren han yi ge nu ren dao Have one cl- m and one cl- come 公 園 散步 公 園 有 一 棵 大 樹 gueng uan san bu Gueng uan you yi ke da shu. . park take a walk Park have one cl- big tree 樹 枝 上 有 一 窩 鳥 母 鳥 Shu zhr shang you yi uo niao. Mu niao tree branch top have one cl- bird Mother bird 飛在 鳥 窩 上 想 教 小 鳥 飛 fei zai niao wo shang. Xiang jiao xiao niao fei. fly bird nest top want teach small bird fly (A man and a woman took a walk in the park. There was a big tree in the park. On top of the tree there was a bird nest. Mother bird flying above the bird nest tried to teach the little birds to fly.)
6.	Hierarchical structure, multiple embedded complex events which are themselves temporally and/or causally connected	有 一 個 男 人 和 一 個 女 人 到 You yi ge nan ren han yi ge nu ren dao Have one cl- man and one cl- woman come 公 園 散步 看 到 公 園 有 一 棵 大 gueng uan san bu. Kan dao gueng uan you yi ke da park take a walk See Park have one cl- big 樹 樹 枝 上 有 一 窩 鳥 shu. Shu zhr shang you yi wo niao. tree tree branch top have one cl- bird 母 鳥 飛在 鳥 窩 上 想 教 Mu niao fei zai niao wo shang. Xiang jiao Mother bird fly above bird nest top want teach 小 鳥 飛 小 鳥 太 小 風 太 大 xiao niao fei. Xiao niao tai xiao. Feng tai da. small bird fly Small bird too small wind too big 結 果 小 鳥 跌 到 地 上 Jie guo xiao niao dien dao di shang. as a result small bird fall to ground (A man and a woman took a walk in the park. They saw a big tree in the park. On top of the tree there was a bird nest. Mother bird flying above the bird nest tried to teach the little birds to fly. The birds were too young and wind was too strong. As a result, the little birds fell to the ground.)

Table 8.1(*cont.*) Coding for narrative complexity

7.	Hierarchical structure as in No. 6 with further episodes embedded within episodes	有 一 個男人 和 一 個女 人 到
		You yi ge nan ren han yi ge nu ren dao
		Have one cl- m and one cl- come
		公 園 散步那 個 男人 和 那 個女 人
		gueng uan san bu Na ge nan ren han na ge nu ren
		park take a walk That cl- man and that cl- woman
		因 爲 喜歡 這裡 所 以 搬 來
		yien uei xi huan zhr li. Suo yi ban lai.
		owning to like here therefore move here
		趁 天 氣好 出來 走 一 走
		Cheng tian qi hao, chu lai zou yi zou.
		Weather good out walk a walk
		看 到 公 園 有 一 棵大 樹 樹 枝
		Kan dao gueng uan you yi ke da shu. Shu zhr
		See park have one cl- big tree tree branch
		上 有一 窩鳥
		shang you yi wo niao.
		top have one cl- bird
		母 鳥 飛在 鳥 窩 上 想 教
		Mu niao fei zai niao wo shang. Xiang jiao
		Mother bird fly above bird nest top want teach
		小 鳥 飛 小 鳥 太 小 風 太 大
		xiao niao fei. Xiao niao tai xiao. Feng tai da.
		small bird fly Small bird too small wind too big
		結 果 小 鳥 跌 到 地 上
		Jie guo xiao niao dien dao di shang.
		as a result small bird fall to ground
		(A man and a woman took a walk in the park. The man and woman liked this area, therefore, they moved here. Since the weather was nice, they took a walk in the park. They saw a big tree in the park. On top of the tree there was a bird nest. Mother bird flying above the bird nest tried to teach the little birds to fly. The birds were too young and wind was too strong. As a result, the little birds fell to the ground.)

Table 8.1(*cont.*) Coding for narrative complexity

8.	As in No. 7 with evaluative coda added	有 一 個 男 人 和 一 個 女 人 到
		You yi ge nan ren han yi ge nu ren dao
		Have one cl- m and one cl- woman come
		公 園 散 步 那 個 男 人 和 那 個 女 人
		gueng uan san bu Na ge nan ren han na ge nu ren
		park take a walk That cl- man and that woman
		因 為 喜歡 這裡 所以 搬 來
		yien uei xi huan zhr li. Suo yi ban lai
		because like here therefore move here
		趁 天 氣 好 出 來 走 一 走
		Cheng tian qi hao, chu lai zou yi zou.
		Weather good come out walk one walk
		看 到 公 園 有 一 棵大樹 樹 枝
		Kan dao gueng uan you yi ke da shu. Shu zhr
		See Park have one cl- big tree tree branch
		上 有 一 窩 鳥
		shang you yi wo niao.
		top have one cl- bird
		母 鳥 飛在 鳥 窩 上 想 教
		Mu niao fei zai niao wo shang. Xiang jiao
		Mother bird fly above bird nest top want teach
		小 鳥 飛 小 鳥 太 小 風 太 大
		xiao niao fei. Xiao niao tai xiao. Feng tai da.
		small bird fly Small bird too small wind too big
		結 果 小 鳥 跌 到 地 上
		Jie guo xiao niao dien dao di shang.
		as a result small bird fall to ground
		失 敗 為 成 功 之 母
		" shr bai uei cheng gueng zhr mu."
		Failure is success poss- mother
		(A man and a woman took a walk in the park. The man and woman liked this area, therefore, they moved here. Since the weather was nice, they took a walk in the park. They saw a big tree in the park. On top of the tree there was a bird nest. Mother bird flying above the bird nest tried to teach the little birds to fly. The birds were too young and wind was too strong. As a result, the little birds fell to the ground. Failure is the mother of success.)

From Kemper and Rash (1990). Telling stories: The structure of adults' narratives. *European Journal of Cognitive Psychology* 2, 205–28

Table 8.2 Intercorrelations between cognitive indicators and indicators of narrative and syntactic complexity

	Age	*Digits Fwd*	*Digits Bwd*	*Narrative complexity*	*MLU*	*Complete utterances*
Education	–0.11	0.09	0.38	–0.10	**0.62**	0.25
Age		0.18	–0.06	–0.13	–0.40	**–0.57**
Digits Fwd			**0.44**	0.06	0.04	0.08
Digits Bwd				–0.0	0.23	**0.65**
Structure Level					–0.08	**0.41**
MLU						**0.40**

Only correlations in bold are significant at the $p < 0.05$ level

formal education. To further test this result, we split the sample into the poorly educated group ($n = 6$, 12 years of education or less) and a high education group ($n = 6$; 16 years of education or higher), and performed a non-parametric Mann Whitney U test for independent samples. No significant differences were found between groups ($z = 0.32$, $p = 0.74$). This result must be read with some caution since the sample size was small; nevertheless it does suggest that further research with a bigger sample is warranted.

Discussion and Conclusion

In our data, then, education correlates with syntactic complexity, and that replicates the research results from other studies. Our data suggest that narrative complexity is not correlated with age, supporting the findings of Kemper *et al.* and not the Juncos-Rabadán study. At the same time age does correlate significantly and negatively with complete sentences. This provides further evidence that a measure of narrative complexity could well serve as a measure of cognitive functioning and functional impairment, some of which might be due to dementia. Although all ethnic groups tell stories, there are differences in narrative practices in different ethnic and cultural groups, the fact that age does not correlate with narrative complexity in both our study and the Kemper *et al.* study on elderly European Americans lends support to the usefulness of storytelling as a diagnostic tool of functional impairment particularly among the lowly educated for whom the classroom like tasks typical of neuropsychological assessment are foreign: 'anybody can tell a story'. The next phase would be to study changes in narrative skills in dementia. In order to use stories for measuring cognitive decline independently of aging, we need to show first that cognitive decline has an impact on this level. Clearly, research with larger groups, and preferably additional non-English groups, are needed to further validate narratives as a tool to assess cognitive functioning.

Summary

This chapter investigated the role of narratives as a diagnostic tool in older Chinese in New York City. We focused on storytelling because everyone was expected to be able to tell stories irrespective of their level of education, so a 'breakdown' in storytelling could serve as a useful diagnostic tool. From a Dynamic Systems Theory perspective storytelling requires the ability to integrate various mental representations visual, auditory, and haptic). It was the ability to integrate these abilities which we sought to test. Stories were elicited using the Cookie Theft Picture from the Boston Diagnostic Aphasia examination, using a coding scheme adopted from Kemper *et al.* The results of our study suggest that storytelling – at least within older Chinese – might potentially be a useful diagnostic tool because narrative complexity is not necessarily confounded by education even if ultimately a diagnosis of dementia is to be based on neurobiological factors.

Notes

1. There are a number of causes of functional dependence in old age, typically a combination of acute illness, accidents, and chronic illnesses. Prominent among the culpable illnesses are cognitive impairment due to Alzheimer's disease and other dementias. 'The measure of cognitive impairment by questionnaire or neuropsychological batteries is a key element in the diagnosis of dementia such as Alzheimer's disease, vascular dementias, Lowey bodies, and other causes such as HIV or chronic alcholism' (Gurland *et al.*, 2003).
2. The analysis is complicated because it is not easy to use Western views when analyzing Chinese texts.

Chapter 9

Language in an Epidemiological Study: The North Manhattan Aging Study in New York City

Introduction

Exploring issues about language and aging from a Dynamic Systems perspective this chapter reports on a study which includes several variables that have been mentioned in the previous chapters. Although the data at the time had not been conducted from a dynamic perspective they take into account change over time. It reports on a study which investigated judgments by raters on the different levels of communicational abilities of elderly subjects from three different ethno-racial groups in North Manhattan in New York City in the United States: African-Americans, Latinos, and whites. In order to make the study as culturally and linguistically fair as possible, each subject was matched with a trained rater drawn from the same ethnic and racial group. The aim was to take away some of the basic problems with testing cognitive functioning in multilingual lower education groups, as mentioned in Chapter 6. The subjects from the three different ethno-racial groups were recruited from a clearly bounded geographical area in which the survey was conducted. A survey was used as a basis for compiling an inventory of possible cases of dementia and non-demented elderly persons because surveys have a greater potential to reach subjects who either were in the early stages of dementia or were seeking medical services outside the clearly bounded North Manhattan area (Gurland, 1996).

In comparison to other research on language and aging (see Chapter 3), the present study possesses several unique features. These are (1) the sample size; (2) longitudinal design; (3) global assessments of health and cognitive status; (4) ratings of language performance by independent raters; (5) inclusion of a wide range of ages and levels of education.

Sample size. One of the main strengths of the study is the relatively large number of subjects who participated in it. Most studies on language and aging are based on fairly small numbers (see Chapters 2 and 3). A majority of studies in language in aging are either a series of case studies (Ramanathan, 1997; Hamilton, 1994; Ridge *et al.*, 2003) or a relatively small size of populations (Emery, 1999; Ulatowska *et al.*, 1999). A total of approximately 2000 subjects in a language and aging project at base assessment is unusual. The number of subjects subsequently reduced to just over 900 after 36 months owing to attrition. The number of subjects who remained in the study even after attrition was still relatively large compared to most other studies in language and aging.

Longitudinal design. Unlike other language in aging studies, the research which forms the basis of the chapter followed those who were not lost, retesting each surviving subject 18 and 36 months after base assessment respectively. Because subjects were followed over time and the first test of each subject was used as a benchmark and base line for himself/herself, theoretically, the health and language trajectory of each subject could therefore be mapped over a 36 month period.

Assessments of health and cognitive status. In many studies on aging, information on health status is lacking (Obler *et al.*, 1999). In this study the health and cognitive status were fully documented including vision and hearing factors. A full evaluation of hearing and vision was necessary because these affect many elderly subjects and may compromise the comprehension abilities of aging persons as mentioned in chapter 4. Each subject in this study was given a full diagnostic evaluation and their health and cognitive status documented.

Independent ratings of performance. The study contributes to accumulating research in language and aging because it explored issues about language and aging using different type of language data taken from an epidemiological study. Most research into language and aging has used 'objective' language data, 'objective' in the sense that the language data were produced by each subject and consisted of formal language tasks, naming, narratives and at times interactional data (see Chapters 3 and 4). The judgments with respect to communicational abilities were made by trained raters.

Wide range of age and education. Another strength of the study is that the subjects varied in age from 65 to 90+. Because of the wide range in age the study was able to include a substantial number of the 'oldest-old' (85 and older). Rarely are the 'oldest-old' subjects included in language and aging research. The 'oldest-old' are however becoming a source of increasing interest in aging research (Antonucci *et al.*, 2002), so this chapter will contribute towards enhancing our understanding of the nature of aging in the 'oldest-old' from different ethno-racial groups. The subjects also varied in terms of reported years of education. The striking feature of the study was the inclusion of subjects reporting 0–4 years of education. The inclusion of poorly educated subjects rendered it possible to examine the extent to which the raters' judgments of the levels of communicational abilities of the subjects could have been influenced by the educational status of each subject.

Situating an Epidemiological Study in Language and Aging Research

Although the North Manhattan Aging Project (NMAP) was initially conceptualized as an epidemiological study it can arguably make an important contribution to language in aging research as well. The aim of the following section is therefore to situate the NMAP within studies in language and aging focusing particularly on research into language production. A majority of studies in language and dementia are cross-sectional. The studies typically compare the language production of subjects of different ages (Emery, 1999). The tendency to use cross-sectional designs in research on dementia is unfortunate because dementia is a progressive neurodegenerative disease that affects language performance differentially across time (Emery, 2000). Cross-sectional studies are therefore not necessarily the ideal strategy to use when trying to gain insight into the language trajectory of subjects suspected of suffering from dementia.

There are few empirical longitudinal studies of dementia particularly involving African-Americans, and latinos. The study sought to fill an important gap in the literature on aging: longitudinal studies into language and aging particularly those involving African-Americans and Latinos are rare. One of the most frequently studied languages is Spanish (see Gonzalez *et al.*, 2001). The NMAP was, however, different because by studying African-Americans, Latinos and whites in addition to Spanish speakers it was cross-ethnic, unlike the Gonzalez study which was interested in exploring bilingual issues in subjects with Spanish as a primary language only.

The NMAP study like the Kemper *et al.* (2001) study, is one of the few longitudinal studies. Both the Kemper *et al.* and the NMAP study have one important feature in common over and above that they are longitudinal studies into dementia. In both studies there is a matching of demented and healthy adults. The NMAP, however, differs from the Kemper *et al.* study in one key feature. In the NMAP the subjects were drawn from three different ethno-racial groups: African-Americans, Latinos and whites, while in the Kemper *et al.* study the subjects were English speakers only.

The NMAP can be compared to other studies which have focused on listener / rater perceptions of the voice features of elderly subjects. Larson *et al.*, 1992 present data on listener perceptions of the voice features of elderly subjects in three different age groups (25–39), (60–69) and (70+). The results demonstrated that there were different voice onset times (VOT) for the various age groups. The VOT varied depending on the subjects' age. Their results corroborate the Kemper (1995) review of research into language and aging production which shows that most people can accurately infer the age of the subjects based on the voice characteristics of the subject. The NMAP is comparable to studies reviewed by Kemper on voice characteristics of aging persons because it involves judgments on the language used by aging subjects. The aim of the judgments was not to investigate whether younger subjects could accurately infer the age of the subjects based on the subjects' voice features but to investigate how their rating of the speech of aging subjects varied depending upon education, age and cognitive status (whether demented or not) of the individual subjects, and whether these judgments varied across different ethno-racial groups when the subjects and interviewees were matched for race and ethnicity. In the following section we enumerate the main objectives of the language aspects of the NMAP.

Aims of the Analysis of the Epidemiological Data and Hypotheses

In the analysis which forms the basis of this chapter we sought to address the following questions:

(1) To what extent were there any ethno-racial differences between African-Americans, Latinos and whites in the judgments made by trained raters on the levels of communicational abilities of each aging subject when each subject was matched in terms of ethnicity and race with an interviewer?
Hypothesis:
It is expected that there will not be any statistically significant differences in communicational ability between the three ethno-racial differences when the subjects and interviews are matched for race and ethnicity
(2) To what extent did education influence the raters' judgments of levels of communicational abilities of each subject?

Hypothesis:

It is expected that there will be statistical differences according to education when age is controlled for.

(3) To what extent was memory impairment related to judgments made of each subject's levels of communicational abilities?

Hypothesis:

It is expected that memory impaired subjects will be rated as worse communicators than those who are not impaired.

(4) To what extent did age as a factor influence the raters' judgments of each aging subject's language abilities?

Hypothesis:

It is expected that when education is controlled for, older subjects will be more likely to be judged as poor communicators than younger subjects.

(5) What were the changes in the raters' judgments of the levels of communicational abilities of the surviving subjects retested 18 and 36 months after base assessments respectively?

Hypothesis:

It is expected that after 18 and 36 months respectively remaining subjects' communicational abilities will be rated as poorer communicators than they were at base assessments, and that there would be a linear regression over the two periods of time

Methodology

The NMAP aimed to establish a registry of cases of dementia within contiguous tracts in New York City. The boundaries of the target areas were 155 to 181 Street, river to river in North Manhattan. The research site fell substantially within the domain of Washington Heights (New York City). It was possible to reevaluate the subjects after 18 and 36 months after base assessments because the subjects were recruited from within a clearly defined geographical area. Reevaluations are invaluable in aging research because dementia can only be diagnosed properly longitudinally. In addition, from a DST perspective, we are interested in the process of change rather than a comparison of steady states. There are, however, limitations in carrying out research in a clearly defined geographical area. Findings from such areas cannot be easily generalized to other multiracial communities. Although the findings cannot be generalized some of the hypotheses could be sufficiently robust to be tested in other contexts or indeed internationally (Gurland *et al.*, 1995). The geographical area in which the study was carried out was both multicultural and multiracial. Its residents included Latinos either drawn from or with strong affiliations to the Dominican Republic, African-Americans and white residents. The

Table 9.1 Demographic features of the target area population age 65 and older at beginning of study

Age	Latinos	African-Americans	White	Total
	N = 4068	N = 3507	N = 774	N = 9349
65–74	65.1% (2650)	56.0% (1965)	41.8% (742)	57.3% (5357)
75–84	27.4% (1114)	32.1% (1124)	40.8% (723)	31.7% (2961)
84+	7.5% (304)	11.9% (418)	17.4% (309)	11.0% (1031)
Education				
0–4	32.4% (1317)	8.7% (304)	5.5% (97)	18.4% (1718)
5–11	50.2% (2043)	40.8% (1423)	32.4% (575)	43.3% (4041)
12+	17.4% (708)	50.5% (1771)	50.5% (11,171)	38.3% (4250)

ethnic/racial categorizations which were used in this study were taken from the US Census Bureau at the commencement of the data collection. Sociologically, the geographical area in which the study was being carried out can be defined as a community in transition. Unfortunately, at the time of the data collection the area was plagued by high crime rates and endemic poverty leading to a mass exodus of young white residents who were replaced by younger Latinos (Gurland *et al.*, 1990). Because of the outward migration of the white communities, their percentages were relatively lower than that of African-Americans and Latinos.

The numbers forming the basis of Table 9.1 were supplied by the special tabulations branch of the United States census for the 13 census tracts in which the study was conducted. The whites had the highest mean age, with a majority being 75 years and older. African-Americans were the next oldest, with 46% aged 75 and older, and the Latinos were the youngest group with only 34.9% aged 75 or older. Latinos were the least educated. Over 60% of the whites and about half of the African-Americans reported 12 or more years of education, while only 12% of the Latinos had 12 or more years of education. Because of the relatively large proportion of Latinos with less than 5 years of education, a special educational category of 0–4 years was created. The category of 'poor education' made it possible to explore the impact of this category on language in aging among Latino subjects, an issue we return to later in the chapter. We will also return later to the complications of using education as a factor when we discuss the results of the study.

The subjects who were recruited and assessed were either living at home or had been admitted to nursing homes within the designated 13 census tracts of North Manhattan. The interviews were administered by trained raters at the subject's home or in a nursing home depending on where the subjects were at the time of the study and the place the subjects found most comfortable. The subjects assigned themselves to one of the three groups: Hispanic/Spanish, white or Black/African-American/Negro. The subjects were matched for race and ethnicity with the raters in order to render the screening and assessment as culturally fair as possible. A Spanish-translation of the compendium instrument was prepared by a Spanish-English bilingual with extensive expertise and experience in using the English version if the instruments. The Spanish version was subsequently analyzed and checked for accuracy by two Spanish-English bilinguals experienced in mental testing. Changes were made to make sure that the Spanish version was consistent with the Dominican dialect of Spanish which was widely spoken in the research area. Linguistically, the English items were translated into Spanish and compared for equivalence with the English version. The field interviews were administered by trained raters using laptops in face-to-face interaction. The interviewers made ratings in a laptop which automatically processed the data which were then merged and later analyzed. The scales and outlines of abilities were derived from an interview schedule and the manual on the questionnaire, and inter-correlations of data across the interview.

Training of Interviewers

The quality of the data which forms the basis of this chapter was enhanced by the training the raters received. The interviewers were trained to ask the questions as they were written. They were instructed not to paraphrase the questions. They were also instructed to ask questions in the order in which they were written. Because many elderly people have hearing impairment, the raters were trained to speak slowly and loudly, but not to shout. A manual was prepared by the Center for Quality of Life at Columbia University to assist the raters in the administration of the protocol. Maintaining the subjects' confidentiality was invaluable in order to enhance the quality of the data. A number of key steps were taken to maintain the confidentiality of the subjects. Firstly, the raters were not permitted to conduct interviews with acquaintances or relatives, or anyone who has no direct connection with the research. The data were kept in statistical form only and there was no identification information on the questionnaire. The study was a low risk: by this we mean it did not do any harm to the subjects. The subjects would also not benefit directly from the study. It was expected that those who would be entering the realm of being elderly in future might benefit from more culturally sensitive cognitive and linguistic assessment.

Because the interview protocol covered a wide range of areas including but not restricted to physical, emotional and cognitive function, utilization of services, socio-demographic characteristics, and quality of life, it was likely to be of interest to the respondents. The interviewers were trained to prevent the subjects from unnecessarily extending the interview by adding unnecessary details. Rephrasings of the questions would render it difficult to compare the results between different ethnoracial groups. The approach to the assessment was radically different from the one in Dynamic Asessment in which the support given to the respondents is manipulated and varied to see how much and what type of assistance the respondent needs before being able to successfully answer the question.

The compendium was compiled from the following six widely used protocols in mental testing in aging research: the Kahn-Goldfarb Mental Status Questionnaire; the Short Portable Mental Status Questionnaire; the Comprehensive Assessment and referral Interview (CARE); Cognitive Scale (dementia version); the Blessed Memory-Information Concentration test; and the Mini-Mental State Examination (MMSE). The compendium was designed in such a way as to ensure a smooth and uninterrupted flow of the interviews.

Demographics of the Subjects in the Study

A total of 2104 subjects (30.6% male and 69.4% females) took part at base assessment. All the subjects who agreed to participate were reassessed 18 and 36 months after base assessment. During the second assessment, i.e. 18 months after the first assessment, the number of subjects had reduced to 66% of the base number (1381). After 36 months the number of subjects had reduced to 996 (46%) of the original number of subjects at base assessment because of attrition.

The first aim of the study was to investigate whether there were any communicational differences between the three ethno-racial groups. When the subjects and interviewers were matched for race and ethnicity, judgments of communicational abilities between the three ethno-racial groups were then subsequently compared (Table 9.2).

Just 5.4% (53) of the Latinos, 6.6% (47) of the African-Americans and 3.4% (14) of the whites were categorized as poor communicators: 57.7%

Table 9.2 Communicational effectiveness and ethno-racial differences

	Poor	*Moderate*	*Good*	*Total*
Latinos	53 (5.4%)	363 (36.9%)	567 (57.7%)	983 (100%)
African-Americans	47 (6.6%)	274 (38.5%)	390 (54.9%)	711 (100%)
Whites	14 (3.4%)	137 (33.4%)	259 (63.2%)	410 (100%)
Total	114	774	1216	2104

(567) of the Latinos, 54.9% (390) of the African-Americans, and 57.8% (250) of the whites were judged good communicators respectively. An analysis of the results supported our hypothesis that when the interviewers and subjects were matched for race and ethnicity, differences between the three ethno-racial groups were not statistically significant ($p > 0.10$). Because global ratings of communicational effectiveness did not vary between the different ethno-racial groups when interviewers and subjects were matched for race and ethno-racial membership, we proceeded to test whether age, education, and memory status affected the raters' judgments of the subjects' communicational effectiveness (Table 9.3).

A total of 114 subjects ranging in age from 65 to 90 + were rated as poor communicators. Of the 114 subjects rated as poor communicators 13.3%

Table 9.3 Global ratings of communicational effectiveness and age

Age	*Poor*	*Moderate*	*Good*	*Total*
65–69	8 2.5%	117 36.2%	198 61.3%	323 100%
70–74	19 3.0%	224 35.3%	391 61.7%	634 100%
75–79	16 3.2%	196 39.3%	287 57.5%	499 100%
80–84	23 6.7%	117 34.1%	203 59.2%	343 100%
85–90	21 20.6%	42 41.2%	39 38.25%	102 100%
90+	27 23.7%	36 4.7%	98 11.9%	203 9.6%
Total	114	774	1216	2104

(27) were between 85 and 89, and 20.6% (21) were 90 +. The numbers and percentages of subjects judged to be poor communicators increased with age. The largest percentage of subjects judged to be poor communicators were the oldest, i.e. 90+.

A total of 1216 subjects were judged to be good communicators; of these 198 (61.3%) were between 65 and 69, 98 (48.%) were between 85 and 89, 39 (38.25%) were 90 +. The number of subjects rated as good communicators declined by 49% between the ages of 65 and 69 and 90%+.

After exploring the relationship between judgments of communicational effectiveness and age, we now turn to an examination of the relationship between global ratings of communication and memory status. Memory status was divided into a seven point scale, and the seven point scale corresponded with three different memory statuses.

(1) Extreme / advanced and dominant.
(2) Background / minor.
(3) Trivial / positive.

Subjects within the extreme/advanced/dominant fell within the dementia range of the scale. Subjects within the background/minor range of the scale were categorized as cognitively impaired, but not necessarily demented. Subjects categorized as falling within the trivial/minor/positive memory status range were categorized as cognitively normal (Table 9.4).

The percentage of subjects categorized as poor communicators rises from 3.2% within the cognitively normal group (i.e. those falling within the trivial/minor/positive range) to 54% in the group categorized as impaired and falling within the dementia range (i.e. extreme/advanced/dominant). Within the group categorized as demented (i.e. extreme/advanced/dominant) only 10% were rated as good communicators. The number increases to 30% in those classified as cognitively impaired but not demented (i.e. background/minor). 58% of subjects in the cognitively normal group (minor/trivial/positive) were classified as good communicators. The results of the study illustrate that there was a higher probability of a subject who was demented being categorized as a poor communicator than there was for a cognitively normal subject being rated as a poor communicator. An alternative perspective to adopt is to argue that the results show that even among subjects classified as demented there was still a proportion rated as good communicators, albeit a relatively small percentage. Conversely, the fact that a subject was categorized as cognitively normal reduced the possibility that they would be categorized as a poor communicator.

After exploring the nature of the relationships between age, education and memory impairment with raters' judgments we now examine the

Table 9.4 Relationships between memory status and global ratings of communication

	Poor	*Moderate*	*Good*	*Total*
Extreme	6	6	9	21
	28.6%	28.6%	42.9%	100%
Advanced	15	26	39	80
	18.8%	32.5%	48.8%	100%
Dominant	10	71	71	152
	6.6%	46.7%	46.7%	100%
Background	9	79	98	186
	4.8%	42.5%	52.7%	100%
Minor	12	198	281	491
	2.4%	40.3%	57.2%	100%
Trivial	5	199	422	626
	0.8%	31.8%	67.4%	100%
Positive	6	162	260	428
	1.4%	39.95%	60.7%	100%
Total	63	741	1180	1984
	3.2%	37.3%	59.5%	100%

changes in the judgments when the subjects were assessed after 18 and 36 months respectively (Table 9.5).

Table 9.5 presents data on the question, to what extent the raters' judgments changed 18 months after base assessment among surviving subjects: 56% (64) subjects had been lost to follow-up after 18 months; 15 (30%) of the subjects who were in the poor communication category were still in the same category after 18 months when they were retested; 9 (18%) were now in the moderate category; and 26 (52%) had moved to the good category. At base assessment there was a total of 774 subjects in the moderate category; 271 (35%) were lost to follow-up 18 months after

Table 9.5 Rating of communication after 18 months

Time 1 (Baseline)		*Time 2 (18 month follow-up)*			
		Poor	*Moderate*	*Good*	*(Lost for follow-up)*
Poor	114	15 (30%)	9 (18%)	26 (52%)	64 (56%)
Moderate	774	12 (1.55%)	53 (6.84%)	438 (56.58%)	271 (35%)
Good	1216	16 (1.36%)	95 (7.81%)	707 (58%)	398 (32%)

Table 9.6 Ratings of communication after 36 months

Time 2 (18 months)		Time 3 (36 month follow-up)			
		Poor	_Moderate_	_Good_	_(Lost to follow-up)_
Poor	50	11 (22%)	4 (8%)	10 (20%)	25 (50%)
Moderate	503	9 (1.78%)	35 (6.95%)	299 (59.4%)	160 (31%)
Good	818	23 (2.817%)	100 (12.25%)	360 (44%)	335 (41%)

base assessment; 12 (1.55% had dropped to poor; 53 (6.8%) retained the same moderate category; 438 (56.5%) had shifted to the good category.

There were 1216 subjects in the good category at base assessment; 398 (32%) of these were lost to follow-up assessment after 18 months; 16 (1.36%) had dropped to poor, and 95 (7.81%) to moderate respectively; 707 (58%) retained the same status. The results do not support the hypothesis that the subjects will invariably receive 'poorer' judgments as they increase in age. The results have to be treated with caution because we are dealing with subjects who survived, and thus we do not know how the subjects lost due to attrition might have been judged.

Table 9.6 presents data on the results of ratings of communication when the subjects were retested after 36 months. After 18 months there were 50 subjects who were categorized as being in the poor category. Of these 50 subjects 25 (50%) were lost to follow-up at a time of retesting after 36 months; 11 (22%) of the subjects in the poor category after 18 months were still in the same category after 36 months; 4 (8%) had shifted to the moderate category, and 10 (20%) to the good category. Eighteen months after base assessment there was a total of 513 subjects in the moderate category; 160 (32%) were lost to follow-up interviews; 9 (1.78%) of the subjects in the moderate category after 18 months had dropped to the poor category after 36 months; 35 (6.95%) retained the same category, i.e the moderate category. There were 818 subjects in the good category 18 months after base assessment; 331 (41%) of these were lost to follow-up interviews; 23 (2.8%) dropped to the poor category; 100 (12.2%) to the moderate, and 360 (44%) remained in the same category after 36 months.

The results seem to disconfirm our hypothesis that subjects would necessarily be judged more adversely after 36 months. A relatively large number of subjects remained in the good category for 36 months. Some subjects categorized as moderate after 18 months shifted to the good category after 36 months. One of the most robust indicators of future performance is status after 18 months.

Discussion

The study demonstrates that when the subjects and interviewers were matched for race and ethnicity there were no statistically significant differences between the ethno-racial groups on ratings of language performance. The results are significant given an increasingly diversifying elderly population and the pressures to produce screening instruments which are potentially culturally fair (Tuokko & Hadjistravropolous, 1998).

The results of the study illustrate that education, contrary to our expectations, did not affect the raters' judgments when the subjects and interviewers were matched for race and ethnicity. Although education did not have an effect on the raters' judgments of the language abilities of the subjects, education is known to affect rates of dementia. Based on an analysis of the rates of dementia and the relationship with education data from the NMAP, Gurland *et al.* (1995) show that there were significant differences in rates of dementia between those with 5–11 and 12 + years of education for African-Americans and whites. The differences in terms of amount of education which were significant for the Latinos were between those with 0–4 and 5–11 years of education. In all cases the subjects with fewer years of education had higher rates of dementia than those reporting more years of education. Education is therefore associated with rates of dementia, but is not necessarily linked to judgments about communicational effectiveness of the language used by aging subjects. In spite of the association of education with rates of dementia, education remains a problematic variable because the quality of education may differ between different ethno-racial groups and between different age cohorts.

Memory measures were reported to be related to raters' judgments of language abilities of the subjects. Generally, subjects within the dementia range were rated as poorer communicators than those in the cognitively intact group according to memory measures. The relationship between the judgments on communicational effectiveness and memory is corroborated by research into the relationship between working memory and language. Studies into language production confirm the hypothesis that subjects with reduced working memory capacity produced more simplified syntax, preferring right branching over left branching sentences. There is, however, an anomalous relationship between memory measures and raters' judgments. The anomaly is apparent when we focus on subjects categorized as falling within the dementia range, but still classified as good communicators. The converse also applied. Some subjects categorized as falling within the normal range were also classified as poor communicators. This seems to suggest that there are some individual differences which are still retained even among subjects classified as demented.

The results of our study do not lend support to the view that individual subjects will necessarily continuously decline as they become older. The results demonstrate that some subjects do indeed improve after 18 months, the subjects retain the same level of performance they had after 18 months; when retested 36 months later. At the same time, we have to keep in mind that there could have been a bias in the attrition of participants in the study, in particular for the two retesting sessions: it is likely that those individuals who feel their communicative skills have deteriorated were less willing to participate.

Conclusion

In this chapter, we have sought to argue for the importance of taking into account raters' judgments because while formal tests might probe individual skills such as morpho-syntactic constructions and lexical access, they cannot assess individuals' abilities to compensate for age-related declines in language performance. It is also instructive to recall that with the exception of complaints about word finding, elderly subjects rarely complain about not being able to communicate. This suggests that they are compensating rather well for incremental losses in production and comprehension. While formal tests measure these small losses, the ability to communicate seems preserved at a global level. Ratings by independent raters however, have the virtue of probing for these communicative abilities.

Although the original aim of the project was not to elucidate the dynamic aspects of the developmental processes, the data can indeed inform us about the nature of changes over time and how these are affected by mental decline, education and other resources. There appears to be an indirect relation between cognitive decline and education. The data also show that there is an interactive and compensatory relation between resources: while there are clear indications of word-finding problems in language production, this does not lead to complaints about communicative ability, suggesting a compensatory role of other language-related resources.

The type of testing used in this project was the traditional one in which participants are subjected to a number of tasks and tests and have to perform on their own. As suggested earlier, it might be more fruitful to use methods based on dynamical assessment that can show the potential of participants to carry out tasks of increasing complexity with different types of support. While in language acquisition and learning such support would refer to potential learning, in testing elderly people with cognitive impairments it would be more on reactivating skills learned earlier in life.

As we pointed out in earlier chapters of this book, the world is sociolinguistically extremely diverse. The diversity poses challenges about the validity of the methods of cognitive assessment. In this chapter based on an epidemiological study carried out in New York City, we were able to demonstrate that some of the social biases which may arise when assessing older individuals could be overcome, particularly when interviewers and interviewees were matched for race and ethnicity. The results also showed the complex effects of education on the judgments which raters make about the communicative effectiveness of the informants. The effects of education seem to vary depending on the ethnic group one is focusing on. There were significant differences in rates of dementia between those with 5–11, and 12 + years of education, while for the Latino community the crucial distinction was between those with 0–4, and 5–11 years of education, perhaps because the Latinos generally had fewer years of education than African-Americans. Generally, the fewer the years of education the more likely the informant was to be rated demented than cognitively intact. It is possible that at least from a Dynamic Systems Theory perspective, education may act as a buffer against debilitating conditions because it provides more resources such as more extensive linguistic skills, and a large vocabulary repertoire which may act as a buffer against debilitating diseases, at least in the early stages of the disease. It is also instructive that not every informant who fell within the dementia range was necessarily defined as a poor communicator. There were some informants within the dementia range who were defined as 'good' communicators. The study ends on an optimistic note because some informants in actual fact did improve as they advanced in age. The subjects who improved with age were those who had remained in the study: the results, however, have to be treated with caution.

We would like to thank Dr Barry Gurland of the Columbia Center for Quality of Life for permission to use the epistemological study for linguistic analysis, and for assisting with the statistical analysis.

Chapter 10

Old and New Perspectives on Language and Aging

In this chapter we try to bring together different fields of research on aging and examine them using a number of different prisms including Dynamic Systems Theory, although most of the studies, including the empirical studies which we carried out, were not conducted with Dynamic Systems in mind. Framing our arguments on the basis of Dynamic Systems we have attempted to do two things broadly. Firstly, to examine the nature of the insights we might develop about language and aging, if we view it using Dynamic Systems, and conversely, what insights we might gain about Dynamic Systems when we view it through language and aging. In Chapter 4 we discussed the linguistic characteristics of elderly language users. The ever-growing literature on this topic shows that there are age-related changes in language use and language skills. There are 'periph-eral' changes in hearing, vision, motor control in handwriting and speaking and more critical changes in different cognitive systems that have an impact on language behavior. There is a reduction in working memory capacity which appears to lead to problems in language production and perception. Syntax appears to be relatively invulnerable once memory con-straints are taken into account. There are clear effects of education in many respects: the most likely explanation for these effects is that higher education probably leads to more extensive linguistic skills, with a larger vocabulary and repertoire and more ways of expressing communicative intentions. The amount of change or decline may be similar for people with different levels of education, but the higher educated have more 'in reserve' and accordingly, overt signs of decline will take longer to become apparent. Education and high proficiency might act as a buffer from cognitive decline. Reduced syntactic complexity does not seem to have a direct impact on the comprehensibility of elderly speech. Elderly speech tends to be used as a basis for age-stereotyping and is evident in the use of specific registers in communication with elderly people.

The relationship between aging and bilingualism tends to be much more complicated than might be initially expected. Bilingualism seems to have a variable effect on aging. This effect seems to depend on the nature of the task being carried out. If the bilingual does not have the resources in their first language, then they may not necessarily always benefit from being assessed in their first language. An analysis of the effects of bilingualism on language and aging is complicated by the different types and varying complexities of bilingualism itself (Baker, 2001).

The main focus of Chapter 3 is an analysis of communication with and between elderly people and in particular the use of an adaptive register now generally referred to as 'elderspeak'. The research on elderspeak shows that some adaptations such as clear pronunciation and slower speech rate may be beneficial, while other adaptations, such as the use of diminutives and exaggerated intonation do not lead to better communication and are perceived as demeaning. Several models have been proposed that show how the use of an inappropriate type of elderspeak can lead to a breakdown of communication or miscommunication leading to withdrawal due to feelings of inadequacy and decline on the part of elderly speakers. Communicative demands may render the caring profession excessively demanding contributing to a high staff turnover. Caring for the elderly may be communicatively demanding particularly in some countries in western Europe, and North America and South Africa in which a majority of the care givers are themselves second language speakers with limited proficiency in English, Dutch, or Afrikaans caring for mother tongue speakers of those languages. Because the care givers are second-language speakers with limited proficiency in the mother tongue of the patients, they may have no option but to use a reduced and culturally inappropriate variety of elderspeak. The use of elderspeak, as we pointed out earlier, might unfortunately not be socially and cognitively advantageous to the very elderly persons in their care. Care giving in situations in which the caregiver is a second language speaker looking after an elderly speaker may constitute some of the most protracted encounters between speakers of different languages because care, if it is residential, may literally be a 24 hour job.

In Chapter 4 we presented a model which seeks to integrate the psycholinguistic and sociolinguistic approaches. By aiming to integrate socio- and psycholinguistic approaches to aging we aim to avoid the over-constructivistic tendencies which reduces aging and its effects to a conspiracy of mankind, and denies the link between physical decline and aging. The integrated model also enables us to avoid potential excesses of psycholinguistic research which situates changes in language production and processing in aging to only internal processes. The combination of socio- and psycholinguistic approaches enables us to conceptualize the nature of the complex relationship between decline and social functioning. For example, a decline in skills may lead to a reduction of the ability to use language as a tool to participate in community activities, which then leads to less participation and more decline. A second way of integrating socio- and psycholinguistic approaches is one which enables us to treat a decline in participation not as the result but as the cause of decline. In some of the literature on aging 'withdrawal' is defined as characteristic of elderly persons. The withdrawal may result from the desire not to be bothered further and to be left in peace. Whether or not the elderly persons withdraw may in part be affected by the nature of the attitudes towards aging within that community, as aptly illustrated by Cohen (1998) in his book on aging in India.

Our main line of argument is that physical decline has potential effects on functional skills such as memory performance, speed of processing and attention, which in turn will affect language skills and language use. Language proficiency is seen as skilled behavior and this implies that without regular 'training', skills will decline. In fact, the use of language in context is an extremely complex activity and can be seen as 'top-sports' from a cognitive perspective. To maintain a complex skill, it needs to be activated regularly. This is what renders elderspeak harmful: when elderly people are spoken to in a restricted register, they will not have a chance to use language in all its complexity and may gradually lose the more advanced aspects of the skills. Such a decline will show in the way language is used, which in turn can be interpreted by interactants as a sign of decline, which will then lead to an even further simplified register and so on. To what extent this model is valid in diverse cultural contexts we don't know. Whether we will ever be able to quantify the relations between components of the model in such a way that the model can have predictive value is not clear. At the moment its main function is to enhance awareness of the role of interaction in the maintenance of language skills. This line of research is relevant not only in language research but in allied health studies as well, particularly nursing care for the elderly. Care may take different forms, physical, therapeutic and interactional. If caring is in part interactionally accomplished, an analysis of the nature of interaction in care can shed insight into how care is conversationally accomplished 'from moment to moment, situation to situation in a tantalizingly unpredictable drama of continuous care and conflict' (Makoni & Makoe 2001:151) An analysis of the discourses of caring will also provide us with important insights into a special kind of institutional and professional discourse, the discourse of the 'total institution' as we strive to understand the nature of the linguistic environment of aging (Goffman, 1961, Hamilton, 1994;

Ramanathan, 1997). The concept of total institution was coined by Goffman (1961). Under total institutions Goffman includes hospitals and prisons and nursing homes.

Our interest in the environment is not restricted to the linguistic environment only but extends to what we may call the pharmacological environment in which aging takes place. By pharmacological environment we are referring to the medical status of the subjects, the nature of the medication they are on, and the type of diseases which currently affect them. Since most elderly persons are usually on a number of different types of drugs, these drugs are more likely to have an effect on their cognitive status and language. Although most psychologists and neuro-psychologists have enquired about the prescribed and non-prescribed drugs patients use, there are few studies which have systematically examined the impact of the medication people are on, their language and cognition. The exact nature of the impact is something which is only gradually beginning to become a subject of analysis (Lorraine Obler, personal communication).

Chapter 6 discussed the literature on multilingualism and aging. So far there is not that much research on this topic, in particular for healthy aging. There is some, mainly qualitative, work on dementia and multilingualism, but hardly anything on the impact of aging on multilingualism or, indeed, the effects of multilingualism on aging. While there is sufficient evidence to show that multilingualism has a positive effect on cognitive development, little is known about its impact on decline. The intersection between multilingualism and aging, particularly in situations of decline, is an important area of study because the population of the aging population is growing and living longer. The aging population also happens to be multi-lingual. Although there is a growing elderly population which is bilingual, there are relatively few studies which have focused on multilingual aging. As far as there is any evidence, it suggests that foreign language skills are well retained in aging, but here general education is likely to be involved as well. A specific aspect of aging and multilingualism is the problems of elderly residents of nursing homes in which the language of the resident and the language of the home are not the same.

In light of the increasing mobility of professionals and non-profession-als in all parts of the world, both voluntary and involuntary, multilingualism will be a factor to be reckoned with in elderly care as evident in some of the traditional immigrant countries like Australia, Canada, and the United States are already experiencing. As indicated, language plays an important role in care, but also in the diagnosis of cognitive decline and rehabilitation. The use of more than one language or even the language that is not the language of the present community is still unusual. There are some signs of awareness of the role of language and the opportunities and perhaps constraints multilingualism might create in the contexts of health care. Perhaps we should not only be focusing on language, even in multilingual situations, but perhaps we should conceptually expand our areas of enquiry to include health literacy. To date most research in applied linguistics on literacy has focused largely, but not exclusively, on educational literacy (Street, 1984). Research on language and aging provides a unique opportunity to extend the line of research in literacy into another domain which potentially affects all of us, health care. Health care affects all of us – because even if we do not have the professional or personal experiences of caring, or seeing loved ones being cared for by others, that we might have to be cared for by others is something that we cannot rule out. Health literacy is being defined here very broadly to include the ways in which individuals interpret and understand health related instructions and discourses. Health literacy has the potential to impact not only language in aging, but health practices generally. For example, the extent to which individuals comply with the medical regimen – a problem frequently reported in the literature – may in part be influenced by how they construe their bodies and health, and understand medical instructions. How they construe their bodies and the medication they take may be influenced by at least two factors: first their proficiency in a second language, or, if the instructions are in their first language, their ability to understand the technical discourse of medicine and pharmacy. In some cases the instructions are not only in a second language but may be relayed to them by a younger person who acts as a mediator between them and the public institutions. That elderly persons may have someone mediating between them and the public institutions is a relatively widespread situation particularly in immigrant communities. If the elderly person is an immigrant she may have to come to terms with novel ways in which their health status is institutionally constructed in the host country. For an analysis of the elderly person's construal of medication instructions, the metaphors used to describe their health status are important. Although basic research into these areas is missing, research into health literacy in so far as it is focused on the elderly in multilingual situations, may provide us with invaluable information which may fill this gap. Conceptually, an analysis of the elderly person's construal of their health status might in part be able to draw upon insights from cognitive linguistics again reinforcing the extent to which research into language and aging is a point of intersection of different sub-disciplines, an argument which Coupland (1997: 28) articulates well when he writes: 'We should resist institutional pressures towards fixed designations . . . and expect to find new insights at the margins of established boundaries.'

Therefore, we decided to include a second part in this book in which we report on some research on aging and multilingualism. We presented three projects on aging in three different communities that do not speak (standard) English. In Chapter 7 we reported on a project on the role of language in health care for African-Americans in the Detroit area in the USA. We discussed various aspects that are specific for aging of this population and we presented some data on the use of different varieties in testing language skills in this group. The data show that the issue of the use of language in testing is a complex one. It is not the case that testing in the language of daily use will automatically lead to better performance. Assessing poorly educated elderly in the language of daily encounters may not necessarily result in an improvement in performance if the participants are not used to being assessed in that language. From a Dynamic Systems perspective, if the testees do not have the requisite resources and experiences of being assessed in their first language they will not necessarily perform better – meaning being assessed in the variety of language which they associate with their first language may not necessarily yield a truer picture of their cognitive status. Whether the testees will benefit from being assessed in a first language may depend upon the experience they have of being assessed in that language irrespective of whether it is a first or a second language. Education and age range effects appear to interact. The striking aspect of the study is that when education is controlled for, elderly African-Americans, particularly those in the 65–74 age group, seem to perform better than their younger counterparts. African-Americans are a diverse group with different migration histories, so whether our findings which drew upon a community from strictly bounded community would be applicable to other African-Americans is an open empirical question.

In Chapter 8 we presented another ethnic group in the USA: the Chinese community in Manhattan, New York. The aim of the project was to find out to what extent storytelling could be used as a tool to assess linguistic and cognitive skills. Theoretically, storytelling involves integrating various mental representations, ranging from sensory imagery (visual, auditory, haptic, etc.), and emotion, to language as reported speech. From a Dynamic Systems perspective the emphasis is on parallel processing rather than traditional serial processing of language. Our argument is that the capacity to tell stories in so far as it is understood from a Dynamic Systems perspective remains relatively robust across the life span. It is assumed that storytelling is valued as a skill in all cultures and that therefore it could be an assessment tool that is less culturally biased than many other tools or techniques. As mentioned before, one of the issues in assessment is the role of education. In the Chinese project this was included in the design since the literature on this is inconsistent. The outcomes show that narrative complexity and age are not correlated, while there is a correlation between age and syntactic complexity. This supports the view that narrative skills are maintained in healthy aging, and can therefore be used as tools to assess cognitive decline as in Alzheimer's disease.

In Chapter 9, the study of language in aging was included in a larger epidemiological study that was carried out with three different ethno-racial groups in North Manhattan in New York City in the United States: African-Americans, Latinos, and whites. The language and aging project was part of a study on the health status of these groups in New York. This study has a number of unique features: It was based on a design in which the participants were matched with same language interviewers so avoiding a between-groups bias. It was also a longitudinal study, which is very unusual in language and aging studies. The data show a remarkable increase of communicative abilities in the group that was rated as poor in the first assessment when tested 18 months later. A similar pattern was found after 36 months: again a considerable number of participants moved to the 'good communicator' category. It is not unlikely that there is bias in the group that survived after 18 and 36 months, but still it is instructive to report that the general pattern was one of increase rather than decline. Our results have to be interpreted with caution because it is possible that we lost the subjects who had declined due to attrition, and remained with those who were showing improvement in aging. The crucial findings from the study are that – at least among those subjects who remained in the study – some of them did improve with time, while others remained in the same status, and others declined with the passage of time, suggesting in terms of Dynamic Systems that the aging persons might show different patterns of development that are at least partly defined by the availability of relevant resources on different levels.

In this final chapter we want to highlight a number of issues that we think will be important for the development of this subfield. We conclude by briefly identifying other theoretical approaches which might be productively used as theoretical lenses through which language and aging might be viewed.

The three studies presented have probably led to more questions than they have answered, but they have made us aware of the many pitfalls in this type of research. The most problematic issues are the role of language in interaction with elderly people, the use of assessment instruments, the language of testing, the selection of participants and the role of education. If some one is multilingual, through which language is their cognitive rehabilitation most effectively administered? Research in bilingual aging has the potential of demonstrating the complexity of language in the assessment of functional capabilities of elderly persons. In this book, bilingualism is construed broadly and bidialectalism is classified as a sub-category of and a type of bilingualism. In the chapter on language use in aging African-Americans (Chapter 7) we reported on one of our studies which examined the effects of doing cognitive assessments of older African-Americans in either African-American Vernacular (AAV) or General American English. The results suggest that the language of the assessment has a significant impact on the performance of the subjects who had between 7 and 11 years of education, but was not significant for those with less than 7 years and those with more than 12 years of education. This implies that in order to get a comprehensive picture of an elderly bilingual person's cognitive capacities (including cognitive plasticity and modifiability) it is necessary to assess them in different languages or language varieties (standard versus vernacular) particularly if they are moderately educated.

Doing assessments in both languages is, however, not a straightforward solution because the scoring has to take into account code-switching: a phe-nomenon frequently reported among bilinguals globally and reported in research in bilinguals. Code-switching may be accepted as a form of speaking in some multilingual societies, and pathological aspects of it can only be assessed by comparing switching behavior with such behavior in the larger community a speaker is part of. Because code-switching occurs frequently, penalizing bilinguals for code-switching in clinical settings nullifies the results of the assessment. What may be unusual may be a clinical situation which mandates that the informants' languages have to keep their languages or dialects strictly separate. According to Haan *et al.* (2002) in the Sacramento Area Latino Study on Aging among individuals tested on the English version of the MMSE, those who code-switched to Spanish had lower scores than those who did not; it would be instructive to know if the code-switching from English to Spanish occurred at those points where patients experienced difficulties in English. Since bilinguals code-switch into their stronger language we might suspect that the Latino subjects in the Haan *et al.* Sacramento study switched to Spanish as their stronger language. Even when the tests are designed and administered in the languages which the elderly person uses and understands, and when code-switching is taken into account during the clinical assessment as illus-trated in the Latino study cited above in the research by Haan and her associates, the assessment may result in cognitively intact persons being misclassified as impaired because notions about language which underpin most neuropsychological tests are frequently derived from the written version of educated analysts' comprehension of notions about language, notions which may be inappropriate when assessing poorly educated older persons who are not literate in a formal sense of the word (Tuokko & Hadjistavropolous 1998).

Bilingual assessment aims to achieve a comprehensive assessment of cognitive capacity. Bilingual assessment is, however, limited because it can not demonstrate whether there is a 'discordance' between capacity and actual behavior, a discrepancy which may arise when the elder is overprotected by the care giver: overprotection may be a type of support which is positive in its intention but negative in its consequences (Makoni & Grainger, 2002). The overprotection may undermine the elderly person's sense of autonomy and abilities resulting in a 'discordance' between potential and actual behavior Although we have focused on how education might result in misdiagnosis due to biased testing there are various ways in which education influences rates of dementia. Gurland *et al.* (1996: 490) identify three possible ways education has an effect on diagnosis:

(1) The 'selective hypothesis', which suggests that persons developing dementia in late life had reduced cognitive resources since early childhood leading to a discontinuance of education.
(2) The 'associational hypothesis', which suggests that 'poor' education goes hand in hand with other mechanisms for inducing dementia; for example, malnutrition exposure to trauma, alcohol abuse, inadequate health care'
(3) The 'educational hypothesis', which suggests that good and life-long education builds and maintains cognitive resources based on robust neurobiological structures and/or behavioral adaptive patterns that compensate for any deteriorative influences bearing upon the brain.

Ardilla *et al.* (2000) report that there are bigger differences between the same age group with different education, than different age groups with the same education. An interesting and illuminating aspect of the Ardilla *et al.* study is that among the lowly educated best performance is reported later rather than earlier in life. Low education results in deferred optimum performance. Empirically, the results of the Ardilla *et al.* study suggest that the age group (31–50) performed much better than the younger age group (16–30), a finding which is consistent with what we report on in Chapter 7.

Diversity in Gerontology

In the closing remarks we want to explore the implications of the diversity which currently confronts gerontology. Gerontology has to address diversity from two distinct areas. Firstly, there are many disciplines which are involved in research into aging, prominent among them being *psychology, health sciences, psychology, (applied) linguistics, anthropology,* etc. Gerontology is thus best construed as a multidisciplinary project. Secondly, because there is no uniform process in aging, people age in different ways and have conflicting social experiences of aging because societies attach varying significations and meanings to aging, Gerontology has to address the social contexts or place within which aging takes place. The nature of aging and the ways of conceptualizing aging are what we are referring to in this chapter as the dual diversity challenges to aging. Dual diversity demands flexibility in ways of carrying out aging research, and indeed in the modes of analysis as well. Disciplinary flexibility becomes even more necessary in contexts in which researchers from different disciplines are collaborating in a common research project. For example, linguists collaborating with epidemiologists could find that the notion of 'language' in epidemiology might not be as sophisticated as they would wish. Epidemiologists might also at the same time feel that subject selection by linguists might be regarded as 'arbitrary' because they do not fulfill the rigor of their inclusion and exclusion criteria as demanded by their discipline. Success in such projects we are arguing require 'disciplined' compromises from the collaborating disciplines.

Research on language in aging may require not only collaboration across different disciplines, but demands that applied linguists draw upon expertise from different subfields of applied linguistics. The general tendency is to view language in aging from a sociolinguistic/psycholinguistic perspective; but it is indeed possible to conceptualize it as a subject area demanding expertise from both language acquisition/bilingualism and language testing. Because of the increasingly large number of elderly people who are bilingual, assessing their 'language' proficiency and cognitive capacity requires some expertise in language testing – as a procedure in carrying out language in aging research.

We are making the claim that language in aging is not only multidisciplinary but it cuts across different applied linguistic subdisciplines as well. Because of the diversity in research orientations between disciplines and differences in aging experiences between groups and between persons, it is not surprising that there is no 'universal' approach, and we feel that given the diversity in disciplinary approaches and diversity in the social contexts in which aging takes place there shouldn't be a 'universal' approach to aging. The approaches to aging have thus rightly tended to be specific to the research discipline and 'ethnic' and 'social' class group in question. The attempt to tailor the research methodology according to the requirements and expectations of the discipline and ethnic, and social class group is ecologically valid because it constitutes a serious attempt to circumvent the educational and cultural factors which confound efforts at carrying out research in aging. Paradoxically, in spite of the diversity in modes of analysis and groups being studied and our argument that there shouldn't be a 'universal' approach to aging, it seems there are at least three 'universal' statements which can be made with some confidence about language and aging. First, that there is no single universally accepted definition for determining functional and cognitive impairment which is applicable across all ethnic groups. Secondly, cognitive capacity is best construed as a continuum rather than in terms of binary opposites. Thirdly, at the very minimum research into language and aging will require some assessment of the medical condition of the research informants in order to gather data on the different types of co-morbid conditions which might adversely contribute to the cognitive status of the research informant. Culpable 'diseases' which negatively affect the cognitive capacity of elderly persons are diabetes, hypertension, stroke and other diseases. The exact impact of such conditions to cognitive capacity and language proficiency has not been systematically analyzed in language and aging research. An assessment of the contributions of such diseases requires the involvement of experts with medical health training.

In the empirical sections of the book we reported on projects in which we experimented with two types of research approaches in aging. In the study into aging in older African-Americans, the focus was on the nature of aging in community based African-Americans. The 'success' of the study depended upon the collaboration with the local communities. The nature of the research question was also in part shaped by the input with the local communities hence the tendency to frame dementias in terms of diabetes, highlighting the ways in which diabetes is a main contributor to dementia. The community-linguist collaboration model which formed the basis of the research into aging in older African-Americans has the advantage that the community is more likely to be actively involved in the research process when they have contributed in shaping the research question. From a narrow scientific perspective, the linguist-community collaboration shifted the research focus. The criteria for selection of research subjects could not be fully determined prior to the study. The research question, in a sense, was the outcome of liaising with interested members of the community. In our research this posed an important challenge because dementias, particularly of the Alzheimer's type, are not high visibility diseases, unlike other infectious diseases. The second model we experimented with in the series of empirical studies we reported in this book was the one which formed the basis of the North Manhattan Aging Project (NMAP). The language and epidemiological study in the NMAP was based on secondary analysis of data. Secondary analysis of the NMAP had its main advantages and limitations. The main advantage was that we were able to access relatively large amounts of data from different ethno-racial groups which had been collected over 36 months.

In this book we have tried to show that language can be viewed as a complex dynamic system and that language development is not a process that stops after puberty or after finishing a course in a foreign language. Language continues to develop over the life span, and the course of the development will depend on the resources that are available to feed that development. Without resources, a system will come to a standstill, and this also applies for language: without use a language will show a natural tendency to decline. At the individual's level, internal and external resources will play a role. Internal resources include memory capacity, attention, motivation, perceptual and motor skills, and existing skills in one or more languages. External resources include the availability of other people to talk to and pressure from the environment to use advanced language skills. The combination of the internal and external resources reflects what van Geert (1994) has called the 'Cognitive Ecosystem' of an individual. It defines what the individual can achieve at a given moment in time. As we have indicated, subsystems (including the resources) interact and changes in one have an impact on others. With respect to language in aging this is particularly clear in the negative spiral that can develop when decline in language skills lead to changes in the way elderly people are treated and talked to. Reduced external resources in the sense of fewer opportunities to use the language optimally may lead to a decline in skills, which in turn lead to both a decline in use of the language and a change in attitudes and linguistic behavior (elderspeak) in the environment. This may be particularly true for settings where elderly people speak a language that is different from their present environment or when the available resources have to be shared by several language systems. The awareness of this negative spiral in communication with elderly people may break this spiral.

Bibliography

Acevedo, A., Loewenstein, D., Barker W., Harwood, D., Luis, G., Bravo, D., Hurwitz, Aguro, H. and Greenfield, L. (2000) Category fluency test: Normative data for English- and Spanish-speaking elderly. *Journal of the International Neuropsychological Society* 6 (7), 760–69.

Albert, M. and L. Obler (1978) *The Bilingual Brain*. New York: Academic Press.

Altmann, L., Kempler, D. and Andersen, E.S. (2001) Speech errors in Alzheimer's disease: Reevaluating morphosyntactic preservation. *Journal of Speech Language and Hearing Research* 44 (5), 1069–82.

Antonucci, T., Okurodudu, T.and H. Akiyama (2002) Well-being among older adults on different continents. *Journal of Social Issues* 58 (4), 617–27.

Ardila, A., Ostrosky-Solis, F., Rosselli, M. and Gomez, C. (2000) Age-related cognitive decline during normal aging: The complex effect of education. *Archives of Clinical Neuropsychology* 15 (6), 495–513.

Ardila, A., Rosselli, M. and Puente, A. (1994) *Neuropsychological Evaluation of the Spanish Speaker*. New York: Plenum.

Artioli i Fortuny, L., Heaton, R. and Hermosillo, D. (1998) Neuropsychological comparisons of Spanish-speaking participants from the U.S.-Mexico border region versus Spain. *Journal of the International Neuropsychological Society* 4, 363–79.

Ashburn, G. and Gordon, A. (1981) Features of a simplified register in speech to elderly conversationalists. *International Journal of Psycholinguistics* 8–3 (23), 7–31.

Astell, A. and Harley, T. (1998) Naming problems in dementia: Semantic or lexical. *Aphasiology* 12 (4–5), 357–74.

Au, R., Joung, P., Nicholas, M., Obler, K.L., Kass, R. and Albert, M. (1995) Naming ability across the adult life span. *Aging and Cognition* 24, 300–11.

Au, R., Obler, K.L., Joung, P. and Albert, M. (1990) Naming in normal aging: Age related differences or age-related changes? *Journal of Clinical and Experimental Neuropsychology* 12 (1), 30.

Baddeley, A.D. (1986) *Working Memory: Theory and Practice*. Oxford: Oxford University Press.

Baddeley, A.D (1988) The Central Executive: A concept and some misconceptions. *Journal of the International Neuropsychological Society* 195, 158–73.

Baddeley, A. (1990) *Human Memory: Theory and Practice*. Hove: Erlbaum.

Bahrick, H. (1984) Fifty years of second language attrition: Implications for programmatic research. *Modern Language Journal* 68, 105–18.

Baker, C. (2001) *Foundations of Bilingual Education and Bilingualism*. Clevedon: Multilingual Matters.

Baker, R. (1995) Communicative needs and bilingualism in elderly Australians of six ethnic backgrounds. *Australian Journal of Ageing* 14 (2), 81–8.

Baker, R. (1996) Language testing and the assessment of dementia in second language settings: A case study. *Language Testing* 13, 33–54.

Balota, D.A., Watson, J.M., Duchek, J.M. and Ferraro, F. (1999) Cross-modal semantic and homograph priming in healthy young, healthy old, and in Alzheimer's disease individuals. *Journal of the International Neuropsychological Society* 5 (7), 626–40.

Barresi, B., Nicholas, M., Connor, L.T., Obler, L. and Albert, M. (2000) Semantic degradation and lexical access in age-related naming failures. *Aging, Neuropsychology and Cognition* 7 (3), 169–78.

Barresi, B., Obler, L.K., Au, R. and Albert, M. (1999) Language-related factors influencing naming in adulthood. In H. Hamilton (ed.) *Language and Communication in Old Age: Multidisciplinary Perspectives.* New York: Garland.

Bartolucci, G., Henwood, K., Ryan, E.B. and Howard, G. (1986) Psycholinguistic and social psychological components of communication by and with the elderly *Language and Communication* 6 (1–2), 1–24.

Baugh, J. (1999a) *Out of the Mouths of Slaves: African American Language and Educational Malpractice.* Austin: University of Texas Press.

Baugh, J. (1999b) *Black Street Speech.* Austin: University of Texas Press.

Baugh, J. (2004) Linguistic Profiling. In S. Makoni *et al.* (eds) *Black Linguistics: Language, Society and Politics in Africa and the Americas.* London: Routledge.

Bayles, K. and Kaszniak, A. (1987) *Communication and Cognition in Normal Aging and Dementia.* Boston: Little.

Bell, E., Chenery, H. and Ingram, J. (2001) Semantic priming in Alzheimer's disease: Evidence for dissociation of automatic and attentional processes. *Brain and Language* 76 (2), 130–44.

Benton, A. and Hamsher, K. (1989) *Multilingual Aphasia Examination.* Lutz: Psychological Assessment Resources.

Benton, A., Sivan, K., Hamsher, K., Nills, R. and Spreen, O. (1994) *Contributions to Neuropsychological Assessment: A Clininal Manual.* New York: Oxford University Press.

Berman, R. and Slobin, D. (1994) *Relating Events in Narrative: A Crosslinguistic Developmental Study.* Hillsdale, NJ: Lawrence Erlbaum.

Bialystok, E., Craik, F. and Klein, R. (2004) Bilingualism, aging, and cognitive control: Evidence from the Simon Task. *Psychology & Aging* 19 (2), 290–303.

Bickel, C., Pantel, J., Eysenbach, K. and Schroder, J. (2000) Syntactic comprehension deficits in Alzheimer's disease. *Brain and Language* 71 (3), 432–48.

Bieman-Copland, S. and Ryan, E.B (1998) Age-biased interpretation of memory successes and failures in adulthood. *Journals of Gerontology Series B: Psychological Sciences and Social Sciences* 53 (2), 105–11.

Bieman-Copland, S and Ryan, E.B. (2001) Social perceptions of failures in memory monitoring. *Psychology and Aging* 16 (2), 357–61.

Bleathman, C. and Morton, I. (1994) Validation therapy: Extracts from 20 groups with dementia sufferers. *Journal of Advanced Nursing* 17, 658–66.

Borson, S., Brush, M., Gil, E. and Scanlan, J. (1999) The Clock Drawing Test: Utility for dementia detection in multiethnic elders. *Journals of Gerontology Series A: Biological Sciences and Medical Sciences* 54 (11), 534–40.

Bortfeld, H., Leon, S., Bloom, J., Schober, S. and Brennen, S. (2001) Disfluency rates in conversation: Effects of age, relationship, topic, role and gender. *Language and Speech* 44, 123–47.

Bosma, H., van Boxtel, M.P.J., Ponds, R.W.H.M., Houx, P.J.H. and Jolles, J. (2003) Education and age-related cognitive decline: The contribution of mental workload. *Educational Gerontology* 29, 165–73.

Botvin, G. and Sutton-Smith, B. (1977) The development of structural complexity in children's narratives. *Developmental Psychology* 13, 377–588.

Brebion, G. (2003) Working memory, language comprehension, and aging: Four experiments to understand the deficit. *Experimental Aging Research* 29 (3), 269–301.

Brice, A. (2002) *The Hispanic Child: Speech, Language, Culture and Education*. Boston: Allen & Beacon.

Brigman, S. and Cherry, K.E. (2002) Age and skilled performance: Contributions of working memory and processing speed. *Brain and Cognition* 50, 242–56.

Browman, C. and Goldstein, L. (1990) Gestural specification using dynamically-defined articulatory structures. *Journal of Phonetics* 18 (3), 299–320.

Browman, C. and Goldstein, L. (1995) Dynamics and articulatory phonology. In R. Port and T. van Gelder (eds) *Mind as Motion: Explorations in the Dynamics of Cognition*. Cambridge, MA: Bradford.

Brown, A. and Ferrara, R. (1985) Diagnosing zones of proximal development. In J. Wertsch (ed.) *Culture, Communication and Cognition: Vygotskian Perspectives*. Cambridge: Cambridge University Press.

Burke, D. and Mackay, D. (1994) Review of 'The Handbook of Aging and Cognition'. *Contemporary Psychology* 39 (3), 263–64.

Burke, D, Mackay, D. and James, L. (2000) Theoretical approaches to language and aging. In T. Perfect and E. Maylor (eds) *Models of Cognitive Aging*. Oxford: Oxford University Press.

Burke, D., MacKay, D., Worthley, J. and Wade, E. (1991) On the tip of the tongue – What causes word finding failures in young and older adults. *Journal of Memory and Language* 30 (5), 542–79.

Cameli, L. and Phillips, N. (2000) Age-related differences in semantic priming: Evidence from event-related brain potentials. *Brain and Cognition* 43 (1–3), 69–73.

Chen, Y. and King, B. (2002) Intra- and intergenerational communication satisfaction as a function of an individual's age and age stereoypes. *International Journal of Behavioral Development* 26, 562–70.

Clyne, M. (1977) Bilingualism in the elderly. *Talanya* 4, 45–65.

Clyne, M. (1982) *Multilingual Australia: Resources, Needs, Policies*. Melbourne: River Seine Publishers.

Cohen, G. and Faulkner, D. (1986) Does 'Elderspeak' work? The effect of intonation and stress on comprehension and recall of spoken discourse in old age. *Language and Communication* 6, 1–2.

Cohen, L. (1998) *No Aging in India: Alzheimer's, the Bad Family, and Other Modern Things*. Berkeley, CA, Los Angeles and London: University of California Press.

Colombo, L., Brivio, C. and Benaglio, I. (2000) Alzheimer patients' ability to read words with irregular stress. *Cortex* 36 (5), 703–14.

Coupland, N. (1997) Language, ageing and ageism: A project for applied linguistics? *International Journal of Applied Linguistics* 7 (1), 26–48.

Coupland, N., Coupland, J. and Giles, H. (1991) *Language, Society and the Elderly*. Oxford: Blackwell.

Coupland, J., Coupland, N., Giles, H. and Wiemann, J. (1988) 'My Life in Your Hands': Processes of self-disclosure in intergenerational talk. In N. Coupland (ed.) *Styles of Discourse*. London: Croom Helm.

Craik, F. and Byrd, M. (1982) Aging and cognitive deficits: The role of attentional resources. In F. Craik and S. Thub (eds) *Aging and Cognitive Processes*. New York: Plenum Press.

Craik, F. and Lockhart, R. (1972) Levels of processing for memory research. *Journal of Verbal Learning & Verbal Behaviour* 11, 671–84.

Croot, K., Hodges, J.R. and Patterson, K. (1999) Evidence for impaired sentence comprehension in early Alzheimer's disease. *Journal of the International Neuropsychological Society* 5 (5), 393–404.

Croot, K., Hodges, J.R., Xuereb, J. and Patterson, K. (2000) Phonological and articulatory impairment in Alzheimer's disease: A case series. *Brain and Language* 75 (2), 277–309.

Crul, T. and Peeters, H. (1976) *Auditieve Discriminatie Test*. Lisse: Swets & Zeitlinger.

Crutchfield, J. (1998) Dynamical embodiments of computation in cognitive processes. *Behavioral and Brain Sciences* 21 (5), 635–36.

Dagevos, J. (2001) De leefsituatie van allochtone ouderen in Nederland: Stand van zaken, ontwikkelingen en informatielacunes. *Voorstudie*. Den Haag: Sociaal en Cultureel Planbureau.

de Bot, K. (1998) The psycholinguistics of language loss. In G. Extra and L. Verhoeven (eds) *Bilingualism and Migration*. Berlin: Mouton de Gruyter.

de Bot, K. (2001) Interaction in the classroom. *Tesol Quarterly* 35 (4).

de Bot, K. (2004) The multilingual lexicon: Modeling selection and control. *International Journal of Multilingualism* 1 (1), 1–24.

de Bot, K. and Clyne, M. (1989) Language reversion revisited. *Studies in Second Language Acquisition* 11, 167–77.

de Bot, K. and Lintsen, T. (1986) Foreign-language proficiency in the elderly. In B. Weltens, K. de Bot, and T. van Els (eds) *Language Attrition in Progress*. Dordrecht: Foris Publications.

de Bot, K., Lowie, W. and Verspoor, M. (2005) *Second Language Acquisition: An Advanced Resource Book*. London: Routledge.

de Bot, K. and Makoni, S. (2005) *Language and Aging in Multilingual Settings*. Clevedon: Multilingual Matters.

de Bot, K. and Schreuder, R. (1993) Word production and the bilingual lexicon. In R. Schreuder and B. Weltens (eds) *The Bilingual Lexicon*. Amsterdam: Benjamins.

de Bot, K. and Stoessel, S. (2000) In search of yesterday's words: Reactivating a long forgotten language. *Applied Linguistics* 21 (3), 364–88.

de Leeuw, I. and Mahieu, H. (2004) Vocal aging and the impact on daily life. A longitudinal study. *Journal of Voice* 18 (2), 193–202.

de Picciotto, J. and Friedland, D. (2001) Verbal fluency in elderly bilingual speakers: Normative data and preliminary application to Alzheimer's disease. *Folia Phoniatrica et Logopaedica* 53 (3), 145–52.

Deelman, B. and Rozema, J. (1981) Nederlandse bewerking. *Short Portable Mental Status Questionnaire*. Groningen, RUG.

Deelman, B. and Rozema, J. (1984) Groninger bewerking. *Short Portable Mental Status Questionnaire*. Groningen, Dept. of Neuropsychology.

de Wilde, I. and de Bot, K. (1989) Language of Caregivers to the Elderly in a Psychogeriatric Nursing Home (in Dutch). Instituut Algemene Taalwetenschap en Dialectologie KUN, Nijmegen.

Dijkstra, K., Bourgeois, M.S., Allen. R.S. and Burgio, L. (2004) Conversational coherence: Discourse analysis of older adults with and without dementia. *Journal of Neurolinguistics* 17 (4), 263–83.

Dillard, J.L. (1972) *Black English: Its History and Usage in the United States.* New York: Vintage Books.

Driessen, G., van der Slik, F. and de Bot, K. (2002) Home language and language proficiency: A large-scale longitudinal study in Dutch primary schools. *Journal of Multilingual and Multicultural Development* 23 (3), 175–94.

Dronkers, N., Koss, E. and Friedland, R. (1986) Differential language impairment and language mixing in a polyglot with probable Alzheimer's disease. Paper presented at the International Neuropsychological Society meeting Veldhoven.

Dronkers, N., Yamasaki, Y., Ross, G. and White, L. (1995) Assessment of bilinguality in aphasia: Issues and examples from multicultural Hawaii. In M. Paradis (ed.) *Aspects of Bilingual Aphasia.* Oxford: Pergamon.

Dussias, P. (2001) Sentence parsing in fluent Spanish-English bilinguals. In J. Nicol (ed.) *One Mind, Two Languages: Bilingual Language Processing.* Cambridge, MA: Blackwell Publishers.

Elman, J. (1995) Language as a dynamical system. In R. Port and T. van Gelder (eds) *Mind as Motion, Explorations in the Dynamics of Cognition.* Cambridge, MA: Bradford.

Emery, O. (1986) Linguistic decrement in normal aging. *Language & Communication* 6 (1–2), 47–64.

Emery, O. (1999) On the relationship between memory and language in the dementia spectrum of depression, Alzheimer syndrome, and normal aging. In H. Hamilton (ed.) *Language and Communication in Old Age: Multidisciplinary Perspectives.* New York: Garland.

Emery, O. (2000) Language impairment in dementia of the Alzheimer type: A hierarchical decline? *International Journal of Psychiatry in Medicine* 30 (2), 145–64.

Finnegan, R. (1970) Oral literature in Africa. London, Clarendon Press.

Fisk, J.E. and Warr, P. (1996) Age and working memory: The role of perceptual speed, the central executive, and the phonological loop. *Psychology and Aging* 11 (2), 316–23.

Folstein, M., Folstein, S. and McHugh, P. (1975) 'Mini-Mental State': A practical method for grading the cognitive state of patients for the clinician. *Journal of Psychiatry Research* 12, 189–98.

Forbes, K,E., Venneri, A. and Shanks, M.F. (2002) Distinct patterns of spontaneous speech deterioration: An early predictor of Alzheimer's disease. *Brain and Cognition* 48, 356–61.

Fox, S. and Giles, H. (1993) Accommodating intergenerational contact: A critique and theoretical model. *Journal of Aging Studies* 7, 423–51.

Francis, W.S. (1999) Cognitive integration of language and memory in bilinguals: Semantic representation. *Psychological Bulletin* 125 (2), 193–222.

Frawley, W. (2004) *Vygotsky and Cognitive Science. Language and the Unification of the Social and Computational Mind.* Cambridge, MA: Harvard University Press.

Friedland, D. and Miller, N. (1999) Language mixing in bilingual speakers with Alzheimer's dementia: A conversation analysis approach. *Aphasiology* 13 (4–5), 427–44.

Fulmer, T. and Gurland, B. (1997) Restriction and elder mistreatment: Differences between caregiver and elder perceptions of the use of restriction in the caregiving relationship. *Journal of Mental Health & Aging* 2 (2), 89–100.

Ganguli, M and Ratcliff, G. (1996) A Hindi version of the MMSE: The development of a cognitive screening instrument for a largely illiterate rural elderly population in India. *International Journal of Geriatric Psychiatry* 10, 367–77.

Garrett, M. (1980) Levels of processing in sentence production. In B. Butterworth (ed.) *Language Production Vol 1: Speech and Talk.* London: Academic Press.

Gasquoine, P. (1999) Variables moderating cultural and ethnic differences in neuropsychological assessment: The case of Hispanic Americans. *The Clinical Neuropsychologist* 13 (3), 376–83.

Gasquoine, P. (2001) Research in clinical neuropsychology with Hispanic American participants: A review. *The Clinical Neuropsychologist* 15 (1), 2–12.

Gathercole, S. and Baddeley, A. (1993) *Working Memory and Language*. Hillsdale: Lawrence Erlbaum.

Giles, H., Coupland, N. and Coupland, J. (1992) Intergenerational talk and communication with older people. *Journal of Aging and Human Development* 34 (4), 271–97.

Giles, H., McCann, R. and Ota, H. Challenging intergenerational stereotypes: Across Eastern and Westen cultures. In M. Kaplan, N. Henkin, and A. Kusano (eds) *Linking Lifetimes: A Global View of Intergenerational Exchange*. Honolulu: University Press of America.

Giles, H. and Makoni, S. (2005) Perceptions of age stereotypes, filial norms, communication behaviors, and communication satisfaction: Young, middle-aged and older US and African adult targets. (Submitted for publication).

Gloning, I. and Gloning, K. (1965) Aphasien bei Polyglotten. Beitrag zur Dynamik des Sprachabbaus sowie zur Lokalisationsfrage dieser Störungen. *Wiener Zeitschrift für Nervenheilkunde* 22, 362–97.

Goffman, E. (1961) *Asylums*. Harmondsworth: Penguin.

Gollan, T. and Kroll, J. (2000) Bilingual Lexical Access. In B. Rapp (ed.) *The Handbook of Cognitive Neuropsychology*. Philadelphia: Psychology Press.

Gonzales, M., Mungas, D. and Reed, B. (2001) A new verbal learning and memory test for English- and Spanish-speaking older people. *Journal of the International Neuropsychological Society* 7, 544–55.

Goral, M. (2004) First-language decline in healthy aging: Implications for attrition in bilingualism. *Journal of Neurolinguistics* 17 (1), 31–52.

Gordon-Salant, S. and Fitzgibbons, P. (2004) Effects of stimulus and noise rate variability on speech perception by younger and older adults. *Journal of the Acoustical Society of America* 115 (4), 1808–17.

Gould, O., Saum, C. and Belter, J. (2002) Recall and subjective reactions to speaking styles: Does age matter? *Experimental Aging Research* 28 (2), 199–213.

Goulet, P., Ska, B. and Kahn, H. (1994) Is there a decline in picture naming with advancing age? *Journal of Speech and Hearing Research* 37 (3), 629–44.

Grosjean, F. (1998) Studying bilinguals: Methodological and conceptual issues. *Bilingualism: Language and Cognition* 1 (2), 131–49.

Grossman, M., Mickanin, J., Onishi, K., Robinson, K.M. and Despisito, M, (1997) Lexical acquisition in probable Alzheimer's disease. *Brain and Language* 60 (3), 443–63.

Grossman, M., Smith, E. and Koenig, P. (2002) The neural basis for categorization in semantic memory. *Neuroimage* 17 (3), 1549–61.

Grossman, M. and White-Devine, T. (1998) Sentence comprehension in Alzheimer's disease. *Brain and Language* 62 (2), 186–201.

Gubarchuk, J. and Kemper, S. (1997) Effects of aging on the production of Russian. *Discourse Processes* 23 (1), 63–82.

Guilford, J.P. (1967) *The Nature of Human Intelligence*. New York: McGraw-Hill.

Gurland, B., Cross, J., Chen, P., Wilder, J., Pine, D.E., Lantingua, R.A. and Fulmer, T. (1994) A new performance test of adaptive cognitive function: The Medication Management Test (MMT). *International Journal of Geriatric Psychiatry* 9, 875–85.

Gurland, B., Ferriera, M., and Makoni, S. (2003) Research draft document.

Gurland, B. J., Wilder, D., Cross, P. Lantigua, R., Teresi, J.A., Barret, V., Stern, Y. and Mayeux, R. (1995) Relative rates of dementia by multiple case definitions, over two prevalence periods, in three cultural groups. *American Journal of Geriatric Psychiatry* 3, 6–20.

Gurland, B. J, Wilder, D., Lantigua, R., Mayeux, R., Stern, Y., Chen, J., Cross, P. and Kleffer, E. (1997) Differences in rates of dementia between ethno-racial groups. In L. Martin and B. Soldo (eds) *Racial and Ethnic Differences in the Health of Older Americans*. Washington, DC, National Academy Press.

Gurland, B., Wilder, D., Lantigua, R., Stern, Y., Chen, J., Kleffer, E. and Mayeux, R. (1996) Methods of screening for survey research on Alzheimer´s disease and related dementia as based on experience in the North American Aging Project. *International Journal of Geriatric Psychiatry* 14 (6), 481–93.

Haan, M., Mungas, D. and Gonzales, H. (2003) The influence of Type 2 Diabetes: Mellitins, stroke and genetic factors. *Journal of the American Geriatrics Society* 51, 169–77.

Hamilton, H. (1994) *Conversations with an Alzheimer´s Patient*. Cambridge: Cambridge University Press.

Hamilton, H. (1999) Language and communication in old age: Some methodological considerations. In H. Hamilton (ed.) *Language and Communication in Old Age: Multidisciplinary Perspectives*. New York: Garland.

Harris, J. (1999) Silent voices: Meeting the communication needs of older African Americans. *Topics in Language Disorders* 19 (4), 23–34.

Harwood, J. and Giles, H. (1996) Reactions to older people being patronized: The roles of response strategies and attributed thoughts. *Journal of Language and Social Psychology* 15 (4), 395–421.

Harwood, J., Giles, H., Fox, S. Ryan, E. and Williams, A. (1993) Patronizing young and elderly adults: Response strategies in a community setting. *Journal of Applied Communication Research* 21, 211–26.

Heath, S.B. (1983) *Ways with Words*. Cambridge: Cambridge University Press.

Heine, M., Ober, B. and Shenaut, G. (1999) Naturally occurring and experimentally induced tip-of-the-tongue experiences in three adult age groups. *Psychology and Aging* 14 (3).

Hendrie, H. *et al.* (1993) The development of a dementia screening interview in two distinct language. *International Journal of Methods in Psychiatry Research* 3, 1–28.

Hendrie H., Osuntokun, B. and Hall, K. (1995) Prevalence of Alzheimer's disease and dementia in two communities: Nigerian Africans and African Americans. *American Journal of Psychiatry* 152 (10), 1485–92.

Herdina, P. and Jessner, U. (2002) *A Dynamic Model of Multilingualism. Perspectives of Change in Psycholinguistics*. Clevedon: Multilingual Matters.

Hermans, D., Bongaerts, T., de Bot, K. and Schreuder, R. (1998) Producing words in a foreign language: Can speakers prevent interference from their first language? *Bilingualism: Language and Cognition* 1, 213–29.

Heyman, A. *et al.* (2003) Estimated prevalence of dementia among elderly black and white population and white community residents. *Archives of Neurology* 48, 594–98.

Hodgson, C. and Ellis, A. (1998) Last in, first to go: Age of acquisition and naming in the elderly. *Brain and Language* 64 (1), 146–63.

Hofstede, G. (2001) *Culture's Consequences*. Thousand Oaks, CA: Sage.

Hulsen, M., de Bot, K. and Weltens, B. (2002) Between two worlds. Social networks, language shift and language processing in three generations of Dutch migrants in New Zealand. *International Journal of the Sociology of Language* 153, 27–52.

Hummert, M., Garstka, T. and Shaner, J. (1995) Beliefs about language performance – adults perceptions about self and elderly targets. *Journal of Language and Social Psychology* 14 (3), 235–59.

Hummert, M., Garstka, T., Shaner, J. and Strahm, S. (1994) Stereotypes of the elderly held by young, middle-aged and elderly adults. *Journal of Gerontology: Psychological Sciences* 49, 240–9.

Hummert, M. and Mazloff, D. (2001) Older adults' responses to patronizing advice. Balancing politeness and identity in context. *Journal of Language and Social Psychology* 20 (1–2), 167–95.

Hummert, M., Mazloff, D. and Henry, C. (1999) Vocal characteristics of older adults and stereotyping. *Journal of Nonverbal Behavior* 23 (2), 111–32.

Hummert, M., Shaner, J., Garstka, T. and Henry, C. (1998) Communication with older adults. The influence of age stereotypes, context and communicator age. *Human Communication Research* 25 (1), 124–51.

Hyltenstam, K. (1995) The code-switching behavior of adults with language disorders, with special reference to aphasia and dementia. In L. Milroy and P. Muysken (eds) *One Speaker, Two Languages. Cross-disciplinary Perspectives on Code-Switching*. Cambridge: Cambridge Univeristy Press.

Hyltenstam, K. and C. Stroud (1989) Bilingualism in Alzheimer's disease: Two case studies. In K. Hyltenstam and K.L. Obler (eds) *Bilingualism Across the Lifespan: Aspects of Acquisition, Maturity and Loss*. Cambridge, MA: Cambridge University Press.

Hyltenstam, K. and A. Viberg (1998) *Progression and Regression in Language: Sociocultural, Neuropsychological and Linguistic Perspectives*. Cambridge: Cambridge University Press.

Irigaray, L. (1973) *Le Language des Déments*. The Hague: Mouton.

Jackson, J. (2002) Conceptual and methodological linkages in cross-cultural groups and cross-national aging research. *Journal of Social Issues* 58 (4), 825–34.

Johnson, S.C., Saykin, A.J., Flashman, L.A., McAllister, T.W., O'Jile, J.R., Guerin, M.B., Sparling, S.J., Moritz, C.H. and Mamourian, A.C. (2001) Similarities and differences in semantic and phonological processing with age: Patterns of functional MRI activation. *Aging, Neuropsychology and Cognition* 8 (4), 307–20.

Johnson-Laird, P.N. *Mental Models Towards a Cognitive Science of Language*. Cambridge: MA: Harvard University Press.

Juncos-Rabadán, O. (1996) Narrative speech in the elderly: Effects of age and education on telling stories. *International Journal of Behavioral Development* 19 (3), 666–85.

Juncos-Rabadán, O. and Iglesias, F. (1994) Decline in the elderly's language: Evidence from cross-linguistic data. *Journal of Neurolinguistics* 8 (3), 183–90.

Kagan, S., Zahn, G. and Gealy, J. (1977) Competition and school achievement among Anglo-American and Mexican-American children. *Journal of Educational Psychology* 69 (4), 432–41.

Katz, S., Ford, A. and Moskowitz, R. (1963) Studies of illness in the aged: The index of ADL, a standardized measure of biological and psychosocial function. *JAMA* 185, 914–19.

Kausler, D. (1994) *Learning and Memory in Normal Aging*. New York: Academic Press.

Kecskes, I. and Papp, T. (2000) *Foreign Language and Mother Tongue.* Mahwah: Lawrence Erlbaum.

Kemper, S. (1987) Life span changes in syntactic complexity. *The Journal of Gerontology* 42, 323–8.

Kemper, S. (1988) Geriatric psycholinguistics. In L. Light and D. Burke (eds) *Language, Memory and Aging.* New York: Cambridge University Press.

Kemper, S. (1992) Adults' sentence fragments: Who, what, when, where and why. *Communication Research* 19, 445–58.

Kemper, S. (1997) Metalinguistic judgements in normal aging and Alzheimer's disease. *Journals of Gerontology B: Psychological Sciences and Social Sciences* 52 (3), 147–55.

Kemper, S., Anagnopoulos, C., Lyons, K. and Heberlein, W. (1994) Speech acccommodations to dementia. *Journals of Gerontology* 49 (5), 223–29.

Kemper, S. and Harden, T. (1999) Experimentally disentangling what's beneficial about elderspeak from what's not. *Psychology and Aging* 14 (4), 656–70.

Kemper, S. and Kliegl, R. (2003) *Constraints on Language, Aging, Grammar and Memory.* Boston: Kluwer.

Kemper, S., Othick, M., Warren, J., Gubarchuk, J. and Gerhing, H. (1996) Facilitating older adults' performance on a referential communication task through speech accommodations. *Aging Neuropsychology and Cognition* 3 (1), 37–55.

Kemper, S., Rash, S., Kynette, D. and Norman, J. (1990) Telling stories: The structure of adults' narratives. *European Journal of Cognitive Psychology* 2, 205–28.

Kemper, S., Thompson, M. and Marquis, J. (2001) Longitudinal change in language production: Effects of aging and dementia on grammatical complexity and propositional content. *Psychology and Aging* 16 (4), 600–14.

Kemper, S., Vandeputte, D., Rice, K., Cheung, H. and Gubarchuk, J. (1995) Speech adjustments to aging during a referential communication task. *Journal of Language and Social Psychology* 14 (1–2), 40–59.

Kempler, D., Almor, A. and MacDonald, M.C. (1998) Teasing apart the contribution of memory and language impairments in Alzheimer's disease: An online study of sentence comprehension. *American Journal of Speech-Language Pathology* 7 (1), 61–7.

Kemtes, K. and Kemper, S. (1999) Aging and resolution of quantifier scope effects. *Journals of Gerontology Series B: Psychological Sciences and Social Sciences* 54 (6), 350–60.

Kjelgaard, M., Titone, D. and Winfield, A. (1999) The influence of prosodic structure on the interpretation of temporary syntactic ambiguity by young and elderly listeners. *Experimental Aging Research* 25 (3), 187–207.

Kline, D. and Scialfa, D. (1996) Visual and auditory aging. In J. Birren and K. Warner Schaie (eds) *Handbook of the Psychology of Aging.* New York: Academic Press.

Kramsch, C. (2000) Social discursive constructions of self in L2 learning. In J. Lantolf (ed.) *Sociocultural Theory and Second Language Learning.* Oxford: Oxford University Press.

Kynette, D. and Kemper, S. (1986) Aging and the loss of grammatical forms: A cross-sectional study of language performance. Language and Communication 6 (1–2), 65–72.

La Tourette, T. and Meeks, S. (2000) Perceptions of patronizing speech by older women in nursing homes and in the community: Impact of cognitive ability and place of residence. *Journal of Language and Social Psychology* 19 (4), 463–73.

Labov, W. *Language in the Inner City* (1972) Philadelphia: University of Pennsylvania Press.

Lantolf, J. (2000) Introducing sociocultural theory. In J. Lantolf (ed.) _Sociocultural Theory and Second Language Learning_. Oxford: Oxford University Press.

Lantolf, J. and Pavlenko, A. (1995) Sociocultural theory and second language acquisition. _Annual Review of Applied Linguistics_ 15, 108–24.

Larsen-Freeman, D. (1997) Chaos/complexity science and second language acquisition. _Applied Linguistics_ 18 (2), 141–65.

Larson, G., Hayslip, B. and Thomas, K. (1992) Changes in voice onset time in young and older men. _Educational Gerontology_ 18 (3), 285–97.

Laver, G. and Burke, D. (1992) Why do semantic priming effects increase in old age? A meta-analysis. _Psychology and Aging_ 8, 34–43.

Lawton, M.P. and Brody, E.M. (1969) Assessment of older people: Self maintaining and instrumental activities of daily living. _Gerontoligist_ 9, 179–86.

Levelt, W. (1993) Language use in normal speakers and its disorders. In G. Blanken _et al._ (eds) _Linguistic Disorders and Pathologies. An International Handbook_. Berlin: Walther de Gruyter.

Levelt, W., Roelofs, A. and Meyer, A. (1999) A theory of lexical access in speech production. _Behavioral and Brain Sciences_ 22 (1), 1–38.

Levelt, W.J.M. (1989) _Speaking. From Intention to Articulation_. Cambridge, MA: MIT Press.

Lezak, M. (1983) _Neuropsychological Assessment_ (2nd edn). New York: Oxford University Press.

Lezak, M. (1995) _Neuropsychological Assessment_ (3rd edn). New York: Oxford University Press.

Lichtenberg, P. (1998) The normative studies project test battery: Detection of dementia in African American urban elderly patients. The Clinical Neuropsychologist 12, 146–54.

Lichtenberg, P. (1999) _Handbook of Clinical Gerontology_. New York: Wiley.

Lidz, G. and Elliot, C. (2000) _Dynamic Assessment. Prevailing Models and Applications_. New York: Elsevier.

Light, L. and Burke, D. (1988) _Language, Memory and Aging_. New York: Cambridge University Press.

Lindenberger, U., Scherer, H. and Baltes, P. (2001) The strong connection between sensory and cognitive performance in old age: Not due to sensory acuity reductions operating during cognitive assessment. _Psychology and Aging_ 16 (2), 196–205.

Lintsen, T. and de Bot, K. (1989) _Language Proficiency in Dutch Elderly People_. Nijmegen: Department of Applied Linguistics.

Linville, S. and Rens J. (2001) Vocal tract resonance analysis of aging voice using long-term average spectra. _Journal of Voice_ 15 (3), 323–30.

Loewenstein, D., Arguelles, T., Barker, W. and Duara, R. (1993) A comparative-analysis of neuropsychological test-performance of Spanish-speaking and English-speaking patients with Alzheimers disease. _Journals of Gerontology_ 48 (3), 142–49.

Lowie, W., Verspoor, M. and de Bot, K. (2005). The application of Dynamic Systems Theory to SLA: What's in it for us? Submitted for publication.

Ludérus, S. (1995) _Language Choice and Language Separation in Bilingual Alzheimer Patients_. University of Amsterdam.

Luria, A. (1973) _The Working Brain: An Introduction to Neuropsychology_. New York: Basic Books.

Luria, A. (1979) _The Making of Mind. A Personal Account of Soviet Psychology_. Cambridge MA: Harvard University Press.

Mackay, D. and Abrams, L. (1996) Language, memory and aging: Distributed deficits and the structure of new-versus-old connections. In J. Birren and K. Warner Schaie (eds) *Handbook of the Psychology of Aging* (4th edn). New York: Academic Press.

Makoni, S. (1997) Gerontolinguistics in South Africa. *International Journal of Applied Linguistics* XXXIV, 167–81.

Makoni, S. (1998) Conflict and control in intercultural communication: A case study of compliance-gaining strategies in interactions between black nurses and white residents in a nursing home in Cape Town, South Africa. *Journal of Cross-cultural and Interlanguage Communication* 17 (2–3), 227–49.

Makoni, S. and Ferreira, S. (2002) Old age and close relations. *International Society for Behavioural Development* 1 (4), 11–15.

Makoni, S. and Grainger, K. (2002) Comparative gerontolinguistics: Characterizing discourses in caring institutions in South Africa and the United Kingdom. *Journal of Social Issues* 58 (4), 805–24.

Marien, P., Mampaey, E., Vervaet, A., Saerens, J. and De Deyn, P. (1998) Normative data for the Boston Naming Test in native Dutch-speaking Belgian elderly. *Brain and Language* 65 (3), 447–67.

Martin, M. and Zimprich, D. (2002) Age-correlated differences vs. changes in intellectual abilities: Can both aspects be explained by the speed variable? *Zeitschrift fur Entwicklungspsychologie und Pädagogische Psychologie* 34 (2), 106–18.

Mayer, M. (1969) *Frog, Where Are You?* New York: Dial Press.

McCann, R., Dailey R., Giles, H. and Ota, H. (2005) Beliefs about intergenerational communication across the lifespan: Middle age and the roles of age stereotyping and respect norms. *Communication Studies* (Submitted for publication).

McCurry, S., Gibbons, L.E., Uomoto, J.M., Thompson, M.L., Graves, A.B., Edland, S.D., Bowen, J., McCormick, W.C. and Larson, E.B. (2001) Neuropsychological test performance in a cognitively intact sample of older Japanese American adults. *Archives of Clinical Neuropsychology* 16 (5), 447–59.

McDowell, I., Kristjansson, B., Hill, G.B. and Hebert, R. (1997) Community screening for dementia: The mini mental state exam (MMSE) and modified mini-mental state exam (3MS) compared. *Journal of Clinical Epidemiology* 50 (4), 377–83.

McGowan, R., Morouny, K. and Bradshaw, P. Managers and eldercare: Three critical, language-based approaches. *Canadian Journal on Aging – Revue Canadienne du Vieillissement* 19 (2), 237–59.

Melendez, F. (1994) The Spanish version of the WAIS: Some ethical considerations. *The Clinical Neuropsychologist* 8, 388–93.

Mendez, M., Perryman, K., Porton, M. (1999) Bilingualism and dementia. *Journal of Neuropsychiatry and Clinical Neurosciences* 11, 411–22.

Menuyk, P. (1977) *Language and Maturation*. Cambridge, MA: MIT Press.

Meyer, B. (2000) Prose analysis: Procedures, purposes and problems. In B. Britton and J. Black (eds) *Understanding Expository Prose*. Hillsdale NJ: Lawrence Erlbaum.

Minsky, M.L. (1977) Frame system theory. In P. Johnson-Laird and P. Watson (eds) *Thinking and Reading in Cognitive Science*. Cambridge: Cambridge University Press.

Miranda, M.R. (1976) Mexican American dropouts in psychotherapy as related to level of acculturation. Spanish-speaking mental health research center. *Monograph Series* 3, 35–50.

Miyake, A. and Friedman, N. (1999) Individual differences in second language proficiency: Working memory as language aptitude. In A. Healy and L. Bourne (eds) *Foreign Language Learning: Psycholinguistic Experiments on Training and Retention*. Mahwah, NJ: Lawrence Erlbaum Publishers.

Morris, P. and Gruneberg, M. (1994) *Theoretical Aspects of Memory*. London: Routledge.

Morton, D., Stanford, E., Happersett, C. and Mogaard, C. (1992) Acculturation and functional impairment among older Chinese and Vietnamese in San Diego County. *Journal of Cross-cultural Gerontology* 7, 151–76.

Mungas, D., Marshall, S., Weldon, M., Haan, M. and Reed, B. (1996) Differential item functioning in the Mini-Mental State Examination in English and Spanish speaking older adults. *Psychology & Aging* 12, 718–25.

Mungas, D., Reed, B. Marshall, S. and Gonzalez, H. (2000) Development of psychometrically matched English and Spanish language neuropsychological tests for older persons. *Neuropsychology* 14 (2), 209–23.

Murtagh, L. (2003) *Retention and Attrition of Irish As a Second Language*. PhD. Department of Applied Linguistics, University of Groningen.

Nebes, R. and Halligan, E. (1998) Alzheimer's disease does not selectively impair decisions about word meaning. *Aging, Neuropsychology and Cognition* 5 (1), 56–62.

Neill, V. (2001) *Cultural Neuropsychological Assessment Theory and Practice*. London: Lawrence Erlbaum.

Neisser, U. (1984) Interpreting Harry Bahrick's discovery: What confers immunity against forgetting? *Journal of Experimental Psychology: General* 113, 32–35.

Nicholas, M., Obler K.L., Au, R. and Albert, M. (1996) On the nature of naming errors in aging and dementia: A study of semantic relatedness. *Brain and Language* 54 (2), 184–95.

Noels, K., Cai, D., Turray, D. and Giles, L. (1999) Perceptions of intergenerational and intragenerational communication in the United States of America and the People's Republic of China. *South Pacific Journal of Psychology* 10, 120–35.

Noels, K.H., Giles, C., Gallois, S.K. and Hung, N.G. (2001) Intergenerational communication and psychological adjustment: A cross-cultural examination of Hong Kong and Australian adults. In M.L. Hummert and J.F. Nussbaum (eds) *Aging, Communication and Health, Linking Research Practice for Successful Aging*. Mahwah, NJ: Erlbaum.

Norman, S., Kemper, S., Kynette, D., Cheung, H. and Anagnopoulos, C. (1991) Syntactic complexity and adults running memory. *Journals of Gerontology* 46 (6), 346–51.

Nussbaum, J., Pecchioni, L., Robinson, J. and Thompson, T. (2000) *Communication and Aging*. Mahwah, NJ: Lawrence Erlbaum.

Nyberg, L., Maitland, S.B., Ronnlund, M., Backman, L., Dixon, R.A. and Nilsson, L.G. (2003) Selective adult age differences in an age-invariant multifactor model of declarative memory. *Psychology and Aging* 18 (1), 149–60.

O'Hanlon, L., Wilcox, K.A. and Kemper. S. (2001) Age differences in implicit and explicit associative memory: Exploring elaborative processing effects. *Experimental Aging Research* 27 (4), 341–59.

Obler, L. (1980) *Narrative Discourse Style in the Elderly*. In L.K. Albert and M.C. Obler (eds). Lexington, MA: Lexington Books.

Obler, L. and Albert, M. (1984) Language in aging. In M. Albert (ed.) *Clinical Neurology of Aging*. New York: Oxford University Press.

Obler, L. and Albert, M. (1989) Language decline in aging. *ITL-Review of Applied Linguistics* 83–84, 63–73.

Obler, K.L., Obermann, L., Samuels, I. and Albert, M. (1999) Written input to enhance comprehension in dementia of the Alzheimer's type. In H. Hamilton (ed.) *Language and Communication in Old Age: Multidisciplinary Perspectives*. New York: Garland.

Ohta, A. (2000) Rethinking interaction in SLA: Developmentally appropriate assistance in the zone of proximal development and the acquisition of L2 grammar. In J. Lantolf (ed.) *Sociocultural Theory and Second Language Acquisition*. Oxford: Oxford University Press.

Orange, J., van Gennep, K., Miller L. and Johnson, A. (1998) Resolution of communication breakdown in dementia of the Alzheimer's type: A longitudinal study. *Journal of Applied Communication Research* 26 (1), 120–38.

Orange, J. and Ryan, E. (2000) Alzheimer's disease and other dementias: Implications for physician communication. *Clinics in Geriatric Medicine* 16 (1), 153–63.

Ostrosky-Solis, F., Ardilla, G. and Lopez-Arango, A. (2000) Sensitivity and specificity of the Mini-mental Examination in a Spanish-speaking population. *Applied Neuropsychology* 7 (1), 25–31.

Overberg, H. (1984) Dutch aged as minority aged. *Australian Journal on Ageing* 3 (4), 30–40.

Overberg, H. (1985) Ageing and ethnic minority status. *Australian Journal on Ageing* 4 (2), 17–23.

Papagno, C. (2001) Comprehension of metaphors and idioms in patients with Alzheimer's disease: A longitudinal study. *Brain* 124, 1450–60.

Paradis, M. (1987) *The Assessment of Bilingual Aphasia*. Hillsdale: Lawrence Erlbaum.

Paradis, M. (1993) Multilingualism and Aphasia. In G. Blanken *et al. Linguistic Disorders and Pathologies*. Berlin: Walter de Gruyter.

Paradis, M. (2004) *A Neurolinguistic Theory of Bilingualism*. Amsterdam/Philadelphia: John Benjamins.

Park, D., Nisbett, R. and Hedden, T. (1999) Aging, culture, and cognition. *Journals of Gerontology Series B: Psychological Sciences and Social Sciences* 54 (2), 75–84.

Pavlenko, A. and Lantolf, J. (2000) Second language learning as participation and the (re)construction of selves. In J. Lantolf (ed.) *Sociocultural Theory and Second Language Learning*. Oxford: Oxford University Press.

Perecman, E. (1984) Spontaneous translation and language mixing in a polyglot aphasic. *Brain and Language* 23, 43–63.

Petersen, R., Jack, C., Yu, Y., Warning, S., O'Brien, P., Smith, G., Ivnik, R., Tangalos, E., Boeve, B. and Kokmen, E. (2000) Memory and MRI-based hippocampal volumes in aging and AD. *Neurology* 54 (3), 581–87.

Pfeiffer, E. (1975) A Short Portable Mental Status Questionnaire for the assessment of organic brain deficit in elderly patients. *Journal of the American Geriatrics Society* 10, 433–41.

Pichora-Fuller, M.K. (2003) Cognitive aging and auditory information processing. *International Journal of Audiology* 42, S26-S32.

Port, R. and van Gelder, T. (1995) *Mind As Motion: Exploration in the Dynamics of Cognition*. Cambridge MA: Bradford.

Portes, A. and Rumbant, P. (1998) *Immigrant America*. Los Angeles: University of California Press.

Pushkar, D., Basevitz, P., Arbucke, T., Nohara-LeClair, M., Lapidus, S. and Peled, M. (2000) Social behavior and off-target verbosity in elderly people. *Psychology and Aging* 15 (2), 361–74.

Radvansky, G. (1999) Aging, memory and comprehension. *Experimental Aging Research* 25 (3), 187–207.

Ramanathan, V. (1997) *Alzheimer Discourse: Some Sociolinguistic Dimensions.* Mahwah, NJ: Lawrence Erlbaum.

Ramig, L. (1986) Aging speech: Physiological and sociological aspects. *Language and Communication* 6 (1–2), 25–34.

Rattcliff, R., Thapar, A., Gomez, P. and McKoon, G. (2004) A diffusion model analysis of the effects of aging in the lexical-decision task. *Psychology and Aging* 19 (2), 278–89.

Ridge, S., Makoni, S. and Ridge, E. (2003) 'I want to be human again': An analysis of the writings of a demented woman. *AILA Review* 16, 156–71.

Ripich, D., Carpenter, B. and Ziol, E. (2000) Conversation cohesion patterns in men and women with Alzheimer's disease: A longitudinal study. *International Journal of Language and Communication Disorders* 35 (1), 49–64.

Roberts, P.M. and Le Dorze, G. (1998) Bilingual aphasia: Semantic organization, strategy use, and productivity in semantic fluency. *Brain and Language* 65 (2), 287–312.

Rosselli, A., Ardila, A., Araja, K., Caracciolo, V., Pardillo, M. and Ostrosky-Solis, F. (2000) Verbal fluency and repetition skills in healthy older Spanish-English bilinguals. *Applied Neuropsychology* 7 (1), 17–24.

Rosselli, M., Ardila, A., Araujo, K., Weeks, V., Volk, L. and Caracciolo, V. (1999) The aging of language in Spanish-English bilinguals. *Archives of Clinical Neuropsychology* 14 (1), 63–64.

Rubin, D.C. (1998) Beginnings of a theory of autobiographical remembering. In C.P. Thompson, D.J. Herrman, D. Bruce *et al.* (eds) *Autobiographical Memory. Theoretical and Applied Perspectives* (pp. 47–67). Mahwah, NJ: Lawrence Erlbaum.

Rumelhart, D.E. (1975) Notes on a schema for stories. In D. Bobrow and A. Collins (eds) *Understanding Studies in Cognitive Science.* New York: Academic Press.

Ryan, E., Anas, A., Beamer, M. and Barjorek, S. (2003) Coping with age-related vision loss in everyday reading activities. *Educational Gerontology* 29 (1), 37–54.

Ryan, E., Anas, A., Hummert, M. and Laver-Ingram, A. (1998) Young and older adults' views of telephone talk: Conversation problems and social uses. *Journal of Applied Communication Research* 26 (1), 83–98.

Ryan, E., Bieman-Coplan, See, S., Ellis,C. and Anas, A. (2002) Age excuses: Conversational management of memory failures in older adults. *Journals of Gerontology* 57 (3), 256–67.

Ryan, E., Bouchard, J. and Norris, E. (2001) 'Communication Aging and Health': The interface between research and practice. In M. Hummert and J. Nussbaum (eds) *Aging, Communication and Health: Linking Research and Practice for Successful Aging.* Mahwah, NJ: Lawrence Erlbaum.

Ryan, E., Giles, H., Bartolucci, G. and Henwood, K. (1986) Psycholinguistics and social psychological components of communication by and with older persons. *Language and Communication* 6, 1–24.

Ryan, E., Hamilton, J. and See, S. (1994) Patronizing the old: How do younger and older adults respond to baby talk in the nursing-home. *International Journal of Aging & Human Development* 39 (1), 21–32.

Ryan, E., Hummert, M. and Boich, L. (1995) Communication predicaments of aging: Patronizing behavior toward older adults. *Journal of Language and Social Psychology* 14, 144–66.

Ryan, E., Kennaley, D., Pratt, M. and Shumovich, M. (2000) Evaluations by staff, residents, and community seniors of patronizing speech in the nursing home: Impact of passive, assertive, or humorous responses. *Psychology and Aging* 15 (2), 272–85.

Ryan, E., See, S., Meneer, W. and Trovato, D. (1992) Age-based perceptions of language performance among younger and older adults. *Communication Research* 19 (4), 423–43.

Sachweh, S. (1998) Granny darling's nappies: Secondary babytalk in German nursing homes for the aged. *Journal of Applied Communication Research* 26 (1), 52–65.

Salthouse, T. (2000) Aging and measures of processing speed. *Biological Psychology* 54 (1–3), 35–54.

Schaie, K.W. (1977) Quasi-experimental research design in the psychology of aging. In J.E. Birren and K.W. Schaie (eds) *Handbook of the Psychology of Aging*. New York: Van Nostrand Reinhold.

Schank, R. and Abeson, R. (1977) *Scripts, Plans, Goals and Understanding*. Hillsdale, N.J.: Lawrence Erlbaum.

Schelstraete, M., Hupet, M. and Desmette, D. (1998) Aging effects on self-paced reading performance. *Année Psychologique* 98 (2), 209–32.

Schmid, M. (2003) First language attrition: The methodology revised. *International Journal of Bilingualism* 8 (3), 239–56.

Schmitter-Edgecombe, M., Vesneski, M., and Jones, D. (2000) Aging and wordfinding: A comparison of spontaneous and constrained naming tests. *Archives of Clinical Neuropsychology* 15 (6), 479–93.

Schneider, B., Daneman, M., Murphy, D. and See, S. (2000) Listening to discourse in distracting settings: The effects of aging. *Psychology and Aging* 15 (1), 110–25.

Scholes, R. and Kellog, R. (1966) *The Nature of Narrative*. Oxford: Oxford University Press.

Schrauf, R. (2000) Bilingual autobiographical memory: Experimental studies and clinical cases. *Culture & Psychology* 6 (4), 387–417.

Schrauf, R.W. (2002) Bilingual inner speech as the medium of cross-modular retrieval in autobiographical memory. *Behavioral and Brain Sciences* 25, 698–726.

Schroots, J., Fernández-Ballesteros, R. and Rudinger, R. (1999) *Aging in Europe*. Amsterdam: IOS Press.

See, S. and Ryan, E. (1995) Cognitive mediation of adult age-differences in language performance. *Psychology and Aging* 10 (3), 458–68.

Seymour, H. (1986) Clinical intervention for language disorders among non-standard speakers of English. In O. Taylor (ed.) *Treatment of Communication Disorders in Culturally and Linguistically Diverse Populations*. San Diego: College Hill Press.

Seymour, H. and Bland, L. (1991) A minority perspective in the diagnosing of child language disorders. *Clinics in Communication Disorders* 11 (1), 39–50.

Seymour, H. and Jones, D. (1981) Language and cognitive assessment of black children. *Speech and Language: Advances in Basic Research and Practice* 6, 204–63.

Small, J. A., Kemper, S. and K. Lyons (2000) Sentence repetition and processing resources in Alzheimer's disease. *Brain and Language* 75 (2), 232–58.

Smitherman, G. (1977) *Talkin and Testifyin: The Language of Black America*. Detroit, MI.: Wayne State University Press.

Smitherman, G. (1981) *Black English and the Education of Black Children and Youth*. Detroit: Wayne State University Center for Black Studies Press.

Smitherman, G. (2000) *Black Talk: Words and Phrases From the Hood to the Amen Corner*. New York: Houghton Miffin.

Snowdon, D. (1997) Aging and Alzheimer's disease: Lessons from the nun study. *The Gerontologist* 37 (2), 150–6.

Snowdon, D., Kemper, S., *et al.* (1996) Linguistic ability in early life and cognitive functions and Alzheimer's disease in late life: Findings from the nun study. *Journal of the American Medical Association* 275 (24).

Spears, A. (1999) *Race and Ideology: Language, Symbolism, and Popular Culture*. Detroit, MI: Wayne State University Press.

Spears, A. (2002) Directness in the Use of African American English. In S. Larehart (ed.) *Sociocultural and Historical Contexts of African-American English*. Amsterdam / Phildelphia: John Benjamins.

Steinberg, R. and Grigorenko, E. (2002) *Dynamic Testing. The Nature and Measurement of Learning Potential*. Cambridge: Cambridge University Press.

Stowe, L. and Haverkort, M. (2003) Understanding language. *Brain and Language* 86 (1), 1–8.

Street, B. (1984) *Literacy in Theory and Practice*. Cambridge: Cambridge University Press.

Stutterheim, C. von (2002) Linguistic structures and information organisation: The case of very advanced learners. Plenary Address, Eurosla Conference, Basel.

Sue, D. and Kirk, B. (1971) Psychological characteristics of Chinese-American students. *Journal of Counselling Psychology* 19, 471–8.

Suinn, R., Vigil, P., Law, S. (1987) The Suinn-Law Asian self identity acculturation scale: An initial report. *Educational and Psychological Measurement* 47, 401–7.

Suzuki, L. and Valencia, R. (1997) Race-ethnicity and measured intelligence: Education implications. *American Psychologist* 52, 1103–14.

Swain, M. (2000) The output hypothesis and beyond: Mediating acquisition through collaborative dialogue. In J. Lantolf (ed.) *Sociocultural Theory and Second Language Learning*. Oxford: Oxford University Press.

Swain, M. and S. Lapkin (1998) Interaction and second language learning: Two adolescent French immersion students working together. *The Modern Language Journal* 83, 320–8.

Tannen, D. (1982) The oral/literate continuum in discourse. In D. Tannen (ed.) *Spoken and Written Language*. Norwood, NJ: Abbey.

Tannen, D. (1987a) *That's Not What I Meant*. New York: Ballantine Books.

Tannen, D. (1987b) Repetition in conversation as spontaneous formulaicity. *TEXT* 7 (3), 215–43.

Taussig, I., Henderson, V. and Mack, W. (1992) Spanish translation and validation of a neuropsychological test battery: Performance of Spanish and English speaking Alzheimers' patients and normal comparison subjects. *Clinical Gerontology* 2, 95–108.

Thelen, E. and Smith, L.B. (1994) *A Dynamic Systems Approach to the Development of Cognition and Action*. Cambridge MA: MIT Press.

Thompson, L., Aidinejad, M. and Ponte, J. (2001) Aging and the effects of facial and prosodic cues on emotional intensity ratings and memory reconstructions. *Journal of Nonverbal Behavior* 25 (2), 101–25.

Toner, J., Teresi, J. and Gurland, B. (1999) The feeling-tone questionnaire: Reliability and validity of a direct patient assessment screening instrument for the detection of depressive symptoms in cases of dementia. *Journal of Clinical Geropsychology* 5 (1), 63–78.

Tulving, E. and Colotla V. (1970) Free recall of trilingual lists. *Cognitive Psychology* 1, 86–98.

Tuokko, H. and Hadjistavropoulos, T. (1992) The clock test: A sensitive measure to differentiate normal elderly from those with Alzheimer's disease. *Journal of the American Geriatric Society* 40, 579–84.

Tuokko, H and Hadjistavropoulos, T. (1998) *An Assessment Guide to Geriatric Neuropsychology*. Mahwah, NJ: Lawrence Erlbaum.

Ulatowska, H., Chapman, S.B., Hill, C., Thompson, J., Parson, S. and Wertz. R.T. (1998) Discourse production in African-Americans with aphasia. *Brain and Language* 65 (1), 236–39.

Ulatowska, H., Chapman, S. and Johnson, J. (1999) Inferences in processing of text in elderly populations. In H. Hamilton (ed.) *Language and Communication in Old Age: Multidisciplinary Perspectives*. New York: Garland.

Ulatowska, H. and Olness, G. (2001) Dialectal variants of verbs in narratives of African Americans with aphasia: Some methodological considerations. *Journal of Neurolinguistics* 14, 93–110.

Ulatowska, H., Olness, K., Hill, C., Roberts, C. and Keebler, J. (2000) Repetition in narratives of African Americans: The effects of aphasia. *Discourse Processes* 30, 265–83.

Ulatowski, H., Olness, G.S., Wertz, R.T., Samson, A.M., Keebler, M.W. and Goins, K.E. (2003) Relationship between discourse and Western aphasia battery performance in African Americans with aphasia. *Aphasiology* 17 (950), 511–21.

US Census Bureau (2000) *National Populations Projections*. Washington DC: Government Printing Office.

van de Ven, H. (1987) 'Ha You Capito?' Bilingual aphasia and code-switching. MA thesis. Department of Applied Linguistics: University of Nijmegen.

Van der Linden, M., Hupet, M., Feyereisen, P., Schelstraete, M., Bestgen, Y., Bruyer, G., Lories, E., Ahmadi and Seron, X. (1999) Cognitive mediators of age-related differences in language comprehension and verbal memory performance. *Aging, Neuropsychology and Cognition* 6 (1), 32–55.

van Geert, P. (1998) A dynamic systems model of basic developmental mechanisms: Piaget, Vygotsky and beyond. *Psychological Review* 5, 634–77.

van Gelder, T. and Port, R. (1995) It's about time: An overview of the dynamical approach to cognition. In R. Port and T. van Gelder (eds) *Mind as Motion: Exploration in the Dynamics of Cognition*. Cambridge, MA: MIT Press.

van Gelder, T. (1998) The dynamical hypothesis in cognitive science. *Behavioral and Brain Sciences* 21, 615–28.

van Heuven, W.J.B. (2000) Visual word recognition in monolingual and bilingual readers. Experiments and computational modeling. PhD dissertation, University of Nijmegen.

van Heuven, W., Dijkstra, T., Grainger, J. and Schriefers, H. (2001) Shared neighborhood effects in masked orthographic priming. *Psychonomic Bulletin & Review* 8 (1), 96–101.

van Heuven, W., Hagoort, P., Dijkstra, T., Schriefers, H. and Swaab, T. (2002) Consistency effects in English visual word recognition: An event-related fMRI study. *Journal of Cognitive Neuroscience* B44, 53.

Verdonck-de Leeuw, I. and Mahieu, H. (2004) Vocal aging and the impact on daily life: A longitudinal study. *Journal of Voice* 18 (2), 193–202.

Verity, D. (2002) Side Effects: The strategic development of professional satisfaction. In J. Lantolf (ed.) *Sociocultural Theory and Second Language Learning*. Oxford: Oxford University Press.

Verspoor, M., de Bot, K. and Lowie, W. (2004) Dynamic systems theory and variation: A case study in L2 writing. In H. Aertsen, M. Hannay and R. Lyall (eds) *Words in Their Places. A Festschrift for J. Lachlan Mackenzie*. Amsterdam: Free University Press.

Vittoria, A. (1999) 'Our own little language': Naming and the social construction of Alzheimer's disease. *Symbolic Interaction* 22 (4), 361–84.

Vygotsky, L. (1978) *Mind in Society*. Cambridge, MA: Harvard University Press.

Wagner, E. (1992) The older second language learner: A bibliographic essay. *Issues in Applied Linguistics* 3 (1), 121–9.

Waters, G., Rochon, E. and Caplan, D. (1998) Task demands and sentence comprehension in patients with dementia of the Alzheimer's type. *Brain and Language* 62 (3), 361–97.

Weltens, B. (1989) *The Attrition of French As a Foreign Language*. Dordrecht/Providence: Foris Publications.

Wertsch, J. (1985) *Vygotsky and the Social Formation of Mind*. Cambridge MA: Harvard University Press.

Williams, A., Ota, H., Giles, H., Pierson, H.D., Gallois, C., Ng, S.H., Lim, T.S., Ryan, E.B., Somera, L., Maher, J., Cai, D. and Harwood, J. (1997) Young people's beliefs about intergenerational communication – An initial cross-cultural comparison. *Communication Research* 24 (4), 370–93.

Williams, K., Kemper, S. and Hummert, M. (2003) Improving nursing home communication: An intervention to reduce elderspeak. *Gerontologist* 43 (2), 242–47.

Wingfield, A. (1992) Language Production in Aging. In F Craik and T. Salthouse (eds) *The Handbook of Aging and Cognition*. Hillsdale: Lawrence Erlbaum.

Wingfield, A., Kemtes, K. and Miller, L. (2001) Adult aging and listening patterns for spoken prose: Spontaneous segmentation versus self-paced listening. *Experimental Aging Research* 27 (3), 229–39.

Wodak, R. (1981) Women relate, men report. *Journal of Pragmatics* 5, 261–85.

Wodak, R. (1986) *Language Behaviour in Therapy Groups*. Los Angeles: University of California Press.

Woo, J., Ho, S., Yuen, Y., Yu, L. and Lau, J. (1996) An estimation of functional disability in elderly Chinese aged 70 and over. *Disability and Rehabilitation* 18 (12), 609–12.

Woutersen, M. (1997) Bilingual word perception. PhD dissertation, Department of Applied Linguistics: Katholieke Universiteit Nijmegen.

Yano, K., Grove, J., Masaki, K. and White, L. (2000) The effects of childhood residence in Japan and testing language on cognitive performance in late life among Japanese American men in Hawaii. *Journal of the American Geriatrics Society* 48 (2), 199–204.

Yi, Zeng and Vaupel, J. (2002) Functional capacity and self evaluation of health and life of oldest old in China. *Journal of Social Issues: International Perspectives on the Well-being of Older Adults*. 58 (4), 733–49.

Zimprich, D. and Martin, M. (2002) Age and skilled performance: Contributions of working memory and processing speed. *Psychology and Aging* 17 (4), 690–5.